PELICAN CROSSING

Dedication

To Alice – dearest Mum

Acknowledgements

A huge "thank you" to Adrian, Peter, David and Jonathan – the young men in my life – for putting up with a wife/mother who was glued to the computer for unreasonably long periods of time. Without their love and encouragement, this book could not have been written.

Thanks also to Tony Collins and Eleanor Trotter at Monarch Books, for their untiring support and professionalism, and their vision to enable *Pelican Crossing* to launch and spread its wings.

DISCLAIMER

All patient and staff names are fictional, having been changed to protect the identities of the individuals concerned.

Readers will appreciate that some of the drugs used will have changed since the late 1970s, but to the best of our knowledge they were the correct drugs and procedures which were used at that time.

Pelican Crossing

The misadventures of
a trainee nurse

HILARY COTTERILL

MONARCH
BOOKS

Oxford, UK & Grand Rapids, Michigan

First published in the UK 2004 by Monarch Books,
(a publishing imprint of Lion Hudson plc),
Mayfield House, 256 Banbury Road, Oxford OX2 7DH
Tel: +44 (0) 1865 302750 Fax: +44 (0) 1865 302757
Email: monarch@lionhudson.com
www.lionhudson.com

Distributed by:
UK: Marston Book Services Ltd, PO Box 269,
Abingdon, Oxon OX14 4YN;
USA: Kregel Publications, PO Box 2607
Grand Rapids, Michigan 49501.

ISBN 1 85424 660 7 (UK)
ISBN 0 8254 6060 3 (US)

British Library Cataloguing Data
A catalogue record for this book is available
from the British library.

Book design and production for the publishers by
Bookprint Creative Services
P.O. Box 827, BN21 3YJ, England.
Printed in Great Britain.

Chapter One

"This is it, Hilly."

My Mum glanced anxiously out of the aircraft window and reassuringly squeezed my hand. Below us lay a world covered in white. Small vehicles scrunched and steamed frigidly through the thin morning sunshine, and I felt a thrill of adventure. Snow was somewhat of a novelty because we had spent the last ten years in Hong Kong's sunny climes.

As the 747 shimmied and swayed, and finally touched down at Heathrow, the entire world seemed to be submerged in white – the harshness of the cold belied by the soft contours of all that was touched by it.

Outside, the air was startingly cold. At this early hour on a January morning in 1979, my life was opening a new chapter. I was at last beginning my own career as a student nurse, and elation and apprehension was vying for top position on the list of emotions I was feeling. My Mum had agreed to accompany me on this journey, and she and I exchanged anxious glances as we stepped out into this new white world.

It seemed incredible that just a few hours previously, she and I had been living in the comparatively warm and luxurious environment of Hong Kong. My father had been promoted to a position with an eminent insurance company ten years previously and I had been privileged to grow up from the age of eight surrounded by en-suite luxury, living on Hong Kong's Victoria Peak. Country clubs, polo ponies, ex-racehorses, and sports facilities that many people can only dream about were the norm.

I had been given the chance to taste the finer things in life. As I had grown up, my parents had given me the opportunity to have amazingly lavish birthday meals; my birthday gifts consisted of beautiful jewellery and lovely, tailor-made garments. I had been allowed to dine at the finest hotels and floating restaurants, surrounded by the awesome spectacle of Hong Kong's dazzling prosperity. I had been prepared for a life amongst the comfortable middle class.

Yet strangely, although I loved the sporting facilities and appreciated all that my parents had taught me, I felt an incredible emptiness which I knew that neither money, fame nor success could fill.

When I was 16, I remember feeling a tremendous restlessness and a longing to find a purpose for my life. I came to the conclusion, having already been given so much materially, that the answer did not lie there.

I decided that the answer must lie in pushing myself very hard. As a consequence, I took to cross-country running. I would go running every morning before walking to the Peak Tram and then walking a further mile to school. I would then follow the journey in reverse in the afternoon, which incorporated very long, steep hills.

At the weekends, I would run a four-mile cross-country course which was used by the Jockey Club to exercise the retired racehorses. It was a beautiful course and often it was one of the few places where I could be alone in Hong Kong's hectic bustle.

It was at this time that I came to the conclusion that I wanted to be a nurse. It seemed to me that this was the ideal career. Perhaps I would find a real purpose for my life in serving other people.

To this end, I applied to the Royal Infirmary of Edinburgh for nurse training. This hospital was chosen because it had a very good worldwide reputation and, although I did not have any relatives in Scotland, my father comes from Aberdeen and we had spent many holidays in the Scottish Borders in previous years.

I attended an interview later in 1977 and was accepted for training in the January following my 18th birthday. I was so relieved – at least I had something to aim for, which would hopefully bring meaning to my life.

The interview itself was extremely daunting. As we entered the hospital through the main entrance, the large hospital crest was impossible to ignore. It depicted a pelican sitting on a nest and feeding her young with her own flesh. It was a most striking symbol of self-sacrifice.

I was led through wide corridors whose tiled floors resembled a never-ending chessboard. The hospital smelled strongly of disinfectant. Numerous people in white coats passed on their purposeful way. The high, arched ceilings gave an almost cathedral-like atmosphere and I felt obliged to step quietly in this most auspicious place.

"Sit here, Miss McIntosh. Matron will be with you shortly."

I sat down on a high-backed oak chair and tried to control the nervousness which was mounting. I knew that this was a life-changing moment. A moment in which my fate was to take a new direction.

My reverie was interrupted.

"Come in, Miss McIntosh."

I was ushered into a small, dark room – its only window obliterated by a fire escape. I sat down on another uncomfortable chair, directly in front of the large oak desk, behind which, in her perfectly starched cap and collar, sat the most matronly Matron one could imagine.

Her entire demeanour was designed to command, if not respect, then certainly obedience. Her posture was as unyielding as the starch, and her eyes as unblinking as a bird of prey.

"Now, my dear, can you tell me why you want to become a nurse?"

I swallowed hard. "I really want to help people. I know that this seems a lame thing to say, but I really want to do a job which will make a difference and help people when they are in need."

Matron smiled thinly. "You understand that nursing is not an easy choice?"

I nodded dumbly. I felt my spirits begin to droop under the gaze.

"The Royal Infirmary of Edinburgh prides itself on its excellent reputation, not only nationally, but also world-wide."

I carried on nodding.

"You will be expected, if we should choose to accept you for training, to uphold the highest standards of behaviour, not only in your professional life, but also in your personal life. Nursing is not just a job, my dear, but it is a way of life. Indeed, it will become your life."

The gravity of this decision began to dawn upon me. Still, I felt that I dearly wanted to make my life mean something. The need to do something worthwhile with my life was overwhelming. I was sure that I would be able to cope with all the hardships and difficulties along the way.

After a few further pleasantries, my Mum was called into the room and Matron informed her that I had been found to be suitable nursing material. I would begin training in the January of 1979.

Following the interview, I returned to Hong Kong to study for my A level examinations. As I was doing so, the need to find a real purpose for my life grew ever stronger. It was at this time that one of my peers underwent a most radical change.

Throughout the first five years of secondary school, Juliette had been a moody and disruptive teenager. She had sometimes aimed her aggression in my direction, as I was hardly the world's most confident person. At times she seemed to be almost overwhelmingly destructive; I was afraid of her, although I tried not to let this be apparent.

It was remarkable, to say the least, when Juliette suddenly seemed to have changed completely. It was as though her life was infused with sunshine. She was smiling and courteous, and seemed to have developed a genuine caring for other people.

Initially, I thought that this must be drug-induced, as drugs were readily available at that time in Hong Kong. After a couple of months, however, as the transformation continued, I felt compelled to ask Juliette what had happened to her. I was totally bewildered when she explained that she had become a Christian and that she had a real and vibrant relationship with Jesus.

I had very little knowledge about religion and did not really begin to understand what she meant. After all, hadn't Jesus been dead for nearly 2,000 years? But I knew that I liked the change that had happened in her life and, if possible, would very much like some of the same.

Juliette suggested that I begin to read the Bible. My parents bought me a King James Bible for my birthday and I religiously read from the book of Proverbs every day. It made no sense to me whatsoever. I felt as though I was chewing on dry chalk – it was getting me nowhere.

It was with all this in mind that I was now embarking on my own life. This was my opportunity to make a contribution to the lives of others and I was determined to succeed. I felt that as long as I did my best and tried to treat others as I would like to be treated, then that should make me a Christian. However, I was soon to find that this was as hollow and void as the sensation which now crept over me. Reality was beginning to strike.

Back at Heathrow, Mum and I waited at the airport for my sister Irene to collect us. Before long, Irene came into view, gliding seemingly effortlessly over the snow and ice in her stilettos, in her own inimitable fashion.

"Hello, darlings. I'm sorry I'm late. The blasted traffic is horrendous this morning."

She swept us along with her dynamic energy, her red hair and flowing elegance parting crowds before us, and we were soon outside, gasping in the startlingly cold air.

Irene drove us to her home in Kew, where we were relieved to rest, because of the jet lag. The following day, we were to make the final leg of the journey to Edinburgh by train.

During that journey, mile after mile of the countryside seemed to be frozen wasteland. The sky seemed impossibly dull and heavy. It did not inspire a feeling of confidence or joy, more a feeling of apprehension and gloom. When we arrived at Waverley Station, we were greeted with the news that it was the coldest day they had experienced for 100 years! What timing!

We took a taxi to our hotel and decided that one item at the top of the shopping list was a hot water bottle. In our quest for this, we trudged out into the now hip-deep snow. For Mum, it was nearer to waist height! Undaunted, we trudged on. The snow was surprisingly unsullied. Perhaps it should not have been surprising, because few people in their right mind would have ventured out on such a day.

We did, however, find one other such soul, who had just made a big impression in a particularly large heap of snow. A muffled voice came from within.

"Sod this stuff!" the voice complained.

In true Florence Nightingale style, I endeavoured to help the lady in question to her feet, meanwhile leaving my Mum perched precariously on a very unstable pile of snow.

"Ta, hen," the snow-lady shuddered. "Ta very much. Could I trouble you for the price of a cup o' tea?"

I cannot remember how we parted from this lady. I have a feeling that she may well have been inebriated and wouldn't have been too bothered if she had spent a longer time face down in the snow. Mum wasn't too impressed. She was freezing.

The following day, the 15th of January, I was due to arrive at the Infirmary and be allocated a room and my uniform. It was very difficult, so different from anything I had known before. I had never felt more alone. I was shown to a coffin-shaped room, with a severe camber. The window looked out on to other rooms in this cold, grey nurses' home which had been condemned for 34 years! They hadn't mentioned this at the interview!

I was instructed to don my new uniform but had great difficulty making up the cap into the correct shape. It was made of cardboard and that, too, was disappointing. My emotions were in danger of making themselves known amongst all these strangers. There were 32 new student nurses in my intake and I felt as though the very ground on which I was standing was so new and strange.

Later on that day, Mum had to begin her long journey home. As she left, I felt bereft. I knew no one, Edinburgh was unfamiliar, the weather was terrible and, to crown it all, I shared my room with a mouse which insisted on running over my feet every time I attempted to use my typewriter!

So this was my brave new world. And I felt like an alien.

Chapter Two

The nurses' home was an amazing rabbit warren, built on a hill, with an alarming tilt from right to left as one looked out of the windows. The corridors were narrow and dark, and the three floors were serviced by an antiquated double-doored lift, which complained vocally whenever it was coaxed into action.

The bathrooms were shared not only by the student nurses but also by an army of cockroaches, which led to many a screeching session. The toilets were in a line of ten cubicles – a far cry from my en-suite amenities at home. The cooking facilities were minimalist. One double-ring electric "cooker" was intended to be used by up to 16 nurses. The heating was oppressive in the winter and non-existent in the summer, and the frames of the windows were so warped that it was impossible to open the windows at all.

In true British fashion, however, my fellow students and I tried to make the best of the circumstances and, as we gathered in our newly-donned regalia, we chatted nervously together, waiting to be introduced to our nurse tutor.

As Miss Gibbs strode into the room, I could feel the corners of my mouth and those of my peers beginning to twitch. Her earnestness, combined with an almost military bearing, which also amazingly incorporated a motherly roundness, was almost too much for my shaky senses to cope with. She was dressed in a tweed skirt and red jumper. She wore sensibly flat shoes and strode around the classroom with great purpose and energy.

As she strode, Miss Gibbs carried a stick with which she pointed to information on the overhead projector. She reminded us that we were embarking upon the most noble of professions. No, it was more than a profession; it was a calling, a vocation. As I listened, I hung on her every word. It was soothing to think that the pain and loneliness I was feeling was actually for some purpose.

"Now, my dears," Miss Gibbs cooed, "as a nurse, you will hold a respected place in the eyes of our society. It is imperative that you always conduct yourselves in a way that is becoming of such respect."

Some of the student nurses began to wriggle uncomfortably in their chairs, and glances shot from one to another across the room. Miss Gibbs then proceeded to talk about legal and social issues.

These were very dry subjects and my attention wandered to the snowflakes which were falling relentlessly outside. Later in the day, we were given some practical training. We were now officially PTS (preliminary training school), which would last for eight weeks before we would be let loose on the unsuspecting public on our first ward placements.

We were instructed in the art of physically lifting patients. These days, manual lifting is virtually unheard of in many NHS Trusts. In the late 1970s, however, we were trained to lift patients manually; indeed most of the student nurse's role was "hands-on", which involved a great deal of lifting and turning patients who were too ill to move themselves, whilst they were in bed.

We were taught the basic skills of reading a thermometer, taking blood pressure, and feeding one another. Never has so much cold custard been consumed by so many, with so much mess!

Probably one of the most memorable sessions, however, was that of resuscitation, for which we had to practise on a mannequin.

I really struggled with this, because every time I attempted to perform artificial respiration, the bag in the mannequin's stomach inflated and made a very embarrassing sound. Only once did I manage to inflate the little plastic bags which were supposed to represent the lungs!

Cardiac massage was another nightmare. I swear that the mannequin had a grudge. Every time I attempted to perform the procedure, the mannequin's chest springs would "boing" and squeak alarmingly; I felt as though the entire class was laughing at my vain attempts to bring life back into this plastic being.

Gradually, the weeks passed and the group began to gel, and then to fragment, as like-minded individuals grouped together for support and friendship. It was during this process that I felt my loneliness even more keenly. The other girls went home at the weekends and went clubbing in the evenings. I was not able to do either, the first for obvious reasons, and the second because I was very lacking in self-confidence and my experiences of drug-ridden Hong Kong had led me to become extremely anxious about such environments.

One Friday, however, one of my peers, Melissa, invited me to her home in Oban for the weekend. It was still freezing; Scotland seemed to be incarcerated in a never-ending winter. As we travelled west, the land was still obscured by this vast whiteness. The novelty seemed to be wearing thin.

Melissa lived in a remote cottage, surrounded by fields and streams. After a cooked breakfast provided by Melissa's mother, we ventured outside, making snowmen and walking for miles. We passed several shaggy ponies, one of which belonged to Melissa. We made an improvised sled and went slipping and sliding down some of the nearby hills. It was great to get away from the austerity of the hospital and to be in a proper home, even if only briefly.

The weekend came to an end and we returned to Edinburgh. I invited Melissa to come jogging with me each evening. We met up and jogged around the Meadows, an area of parkland situated just behind the Infirmary. All went well until a series of attempted rapes dissuaded us from running there again.

Determined to continue with the keep-fit regime, I made my way to the athletics track at Meadowbank Stadium on the other side of the city. I joined a training team three evenings a week and went through a two-hour training session each time, followed by the long walk home. Melissa joined me in this; it was great to have someone to talk to who shared my ambition to become fit. As time passed, however, the demands of the course, and the interests of the other girls, meant that Melissa no longer wished to continue with the athletics training. I can't say that I blamed her.

I was no longer running to try to get fit. It was becoming an obsession for me. It was the only thing in my life that I felt I had any control over. I would force myself to walk and run all that way, day after day, just to try to keep the fear and pain that I was feeling under some sort of control. It was the only way that I felt I could express my frustration at being so inadequate. I didn't understand the other girls in my group. They all knew how to enjoy themselves and yet I was thoroughly disenchanted with the things which seemed to interest them so greatly.

I know that I came across as distant and aloof. It was my only defence. How was I supposed to exist in this alien environment, without anyone I could truly rely on and trust? Letters home were some comfort, but how I needed someone I could talk to who would really understand!

Things began to fall apart. I gave up the vain attempt I had made at cooking for myself. I skipped meals altogether; the only thing I would eat was breakfast cereal. Even then, the milk which I had bought to accompany it was usually stolen from the communal fridge. So dry cereal was the staple diet.

Even then, I believed that I was grossly overweight. My entire self-image began to distort and, having lost a great deal of weight, I began to feel weak and unwell all of the time.

It was in this precarious state that I had the opportunity to work on my first ward. It was Surgical Urology and the ward was run by a nursing sister from the dark ages. Sister McBride was severely short-sighted, owing to an incident which had happened several years previously.

Whilst recovering from a cataract operation, and still in hospital, Sister McBride had leapt out of bed to resuscitate her neighbouring patient, who had suddenly suffered a cardiac arrest. In so doing, she had permanently damaged both of her own eyes. With or without her eyes, Sister McBride was a woman to be feared. She ruled with a rod of steel.

When I walked on to the ward for the first time, this diminutive figure in white was busily ensuring that all the counterpanes were folded back to the same length on each of the beds. The wheels of the beds were all to be pointing in the same direction and the bedside lockers were to be empty of all but a jug of water, one tumbler, and a concessionary vase of flowers. Even the patients were propped at the same angle, with the same number of pillows supporting them, irrespective of their individual needs. All was orderliness. All was controlled.

We "took report" from the previous shift whilst standing at the doors of the ward. We were not allowed to sit or take notes but had to stand with our hands clasped in front of us and memorise each and every detail about each patient. We would be quizzed by Sister at her convenience later in the shift.

My most vivid recollection of this ward was of spending every shift carrying full buckets of urine, saline solution and blood clots from each bedside to the sluice, then returning with an empty bucket into which I had to drain the appropriate catheter bag's contents. Back and forth I would trudge with the heavy buckets, constantly mopping the floors where there had been spillages and trying to smile at the men who were somewhere at the end of the large bags of saline, buckets and rubber tubing.

One day stands out from the rest, however. On this day I was to be introduced to some of the nuances of the Scottish dialect. It occurred one morning on an early shift, whilst I was attempting to help a man out of bed. Mr McCorrigan, a short but stocky man who was recovering from a trans-urethral resection of the prostate, which had occurred several days previously, was becoming increasingly agitated.

He kept insisting: "Gi' me ma wallies, hen."

"I'm sorry, Mr McCorrigan, could you say that again? I'm afraid that I couldn't understand what you said."

Patiently, he tried again. By the fourth attempt, we both decided that it wasn't that important and I proceeded to pivot him round to help him into a sitting position on the side of the bed.

At this point, he began in a stage whisper, "Ma breeks! Where are ma breeks?"

Now he had me completely flummoxed. What on earth were "breeks"?

As I tried to help him move forward a little more, the stage whisper gave way to a stifled scream. Mr McCorrigan's face became pale with indignation and he pulled the bedclothes determinedly about his person. It suddenly occurred to me that breeks meant pyjama trousers.

Now that we were beginning to understand each other a little better, I hastily handed him the pyjama trousers, and dignity was restored. I later came to understand that wallies meant false teeth. Poor man, fancy having to cope with a nurse who doesn't even understand what you are saying with your teeth in, let alone without!

Time passed, and the well-worn path to the sluice continued. One morning late in March, I remember looking up from the bedpan washer (we were now on first-name terms) and seeing the first buds of spring on the trees outside. I had been so preoccupied with the sheer exhaustion of my work that I had failed to notice the little miracle which was occurring outside. At last, winter was losing its grip on Scotland and there was a ray of hope for better things to come.

I don't know why, but something significant happened at that moment. It was as though an enormous amount of pain resurfaced and I suddenly became very angry.

I felt angry because I had spent the last ten weeks in what seemed to be a god-forsaken ice bucket, where I had run miles carrying hundreds of litres of urine and blood clots under the unrelenting gaze of Sister McBride, who seemed impossible to please. I was frightened of the doctors, terrified of the staff nurses, and I felt alone, unsupported and downtrodden.

From that moment, I began to resent intensely the petty-minded exactness of Sister's regime. It seemed to be without reason or heart and, as far as I could see, just doing things a certain way because of tradition did not seem to justify it at all.

On one day, Sister bellowed at me from the top of the ward to enquire why I had not performed some observations. We were one member of staff down and I was doing the job of two minions. The bucket run was interspersed with temperatures, pulses and blood pressures. At that moment, the buckets were winning the day and several were perilously close to overflowing.

To be publicly harangued in this manner was the last straw. I sullenly walked up to Sister and attempted to explain the situation, but she would have none of it.

"Nurse McIntosh, why have you not completed the observations on Mr Colhoun?"

"I am sorry, Sister," I replied, "but . . ."

"Nurse McIntosh, there can be no 'buts' where nursing is concerned. What would have happened to Mr Colhoun if his condition had changed and you had not bothered to notice?"

Sister knew that this was a question which had no answer. I looked at her and very nearly told her exactly what I thought of her military regime and her uncaring attitude. From that moment, I felt my attitude change; I made a vow to myself that I would never treat a colleague in such a way. My fear of Sister McBride turned to disdain and I counted the days until I would be finally free from her rule.

Chapter Three

As the spring sunshine began to make an impression upon the incarceration of winter, life began to improve. I was allocated to my second ward, which was situated on the medical wing. It was Male Medical. It had the added bonus of being adjacent to the Coronary Care Unit, which was the major regional unit of its kind.

The atmosphere on this ward was so different from that of the previous one. Sister Dunstan was young, vibrant, happy and kind. She ran a compassionate ward, where patients were lovingly cared for and valued. At last I had found someone who seemed to be endorsing the values for which I had entered training.

The work on the ward was very hard physically. On a morning shift, two student nurses would spend three hours lifting very large patients into and out of the bath. There were no hoists in those days and the student nurses were expected to perform this very manual lifting whenever on duty in the morning.

It was exhausting and, being well aware of the embarrassment caused to the patients concerned, we always did our best to ensure that their dignity was preserved at all costs. And quite often it did cost. It was extremely difficult to lift someone weighing well over 200 pounds without grunting audibly with the effort. By the end of each bathing session, every muscle would be creaking and complaining, but we were expected to continue as though we were as fresh as a daisy.

Thankfully, the hard labour involved was in some way

offset by the attitude of the ward sister. Sister Dunstan was a capable leader and she had some kindly staff nurses who worked with her. One morning, however, does stand out in my memory.

One of the consultants was on the ward, at the beginning of his round. Sister and the staff nurses were attending, and so were numerous registrars, senior house officers and medical students. As they passed a bed which contained a man who obviously was not under the care of Dr Blairdrie, I noticed that there seemed to be a sad lack of respiratory effort from the bed's occupant.

I stood transfixed by this man's still chest. Not wanting to cause a stir in the middle of the hallowed "doctors' round", I stood for a moment or two longer, just to make sure that he really had stopped breathing. He looked so peaceful – as though he were sleeping.

I wasn't sure what to do next. Should I shout "Cardiac arrest – call the crash team!" or should I try a more subtle approach? Still afflicted with an unrealistic fear of consultants, I sidled up to the nearest staff nurse and said: "Would you please come and look at Mr McEwan? I'm not sure that he is still breathing."

Staff Nurse Murray's eyes began to bulge and she hastily followed me to the appropriate bed. There she confirmed the fact that Mr McEwan had indeed passed away. Fortunately (for me, anyway), this gentleman's prognosis had been very poor and he had not been expected to live. He was therefore allowed to die in peace. We closed the curtains around him and continued with the round.

I was later left in no doubt that a more robust response to my findings would have been more appropriate. The clinical nurse tutor arrived on the ward shortly afterwards and instructed me in the performing of last offices for Mr McEwan. I found this difficult, and every second expected him to sit up and say: "Just kiddin'".

He didn't do this, however, and the stainless steel mortuary trolley came along in due course and trundled Mr McEwan away.

In the afternoon, I nearly became the target of an airborne vase which had been hurled unexpectedly by a gentleman on the right side of the ward. Mr Milligan had been admitted with a terminal brain tumour, an asterocytoma. It was an aggressive and very fast-growing lesion which had caused Mr Milligan to become very ill, very quickly.

I had just walked past the bed and was approaching the laundry cupboard to collect some more draw-sheets for the linen trolley, when the peace and quiet was shattered by the sound of breaking glass.

I spun round to see Mr Milligan flailing wildly in his bed, convulsing and thrashing. His bedside cabinet was thrown to the floor, and a large hole in the window opposite his bed showed where the vase had made its unscheduled exit.

Sister and two of the staff nurses rushed to prevent any further injury to Mr Milligan, and a senior student nurse fast-bleeped the senior house officer to come and administer some sedation. I tried not to get in anyone's way and carried on with the duties to which I had been assigned.

Once calm had been restored and the ward had been cleared of the shattered glass, Sister emerged from the curtains.

"Are you all right, Nurse McIntosh? That was a near miss! The vase must have only missed you by inches."

Carrying that worrying thought with me, I continued with the basic care of my patients. This was the wonderful thing about nursing: you never quite knew what was going to happen next.

Mr Milligan remained heavily sedated for the remainder of the shift and, during the night, he quietly passed away.

The following day was a day off for me, so I decided, with the improvement in the weather, to take a walk to Dalkeith, some seven-and-a-half miles away.

It was a beautiful spring morning; the sun was shining and at last there was a hint of warmth in its cheering rays. There was a scent of warmth in the earth as I began to walk through the more rural outskirts of Edinburgh and, as I passed Arthur's Seat, the breeze had lost its icy chill.

I walked on and began to pass fields in which sheep had recently given birth to their lambs. I stopped to watch the newborn lambs wobbling and bunny-hopping around their mothers. I had never seen this before and the miracle of new life struck a chord in my heart. It was so simple, so beautiful, so funny and awesome.

Reluctantly, I left the sheep to their own business and carried on with my walk. A moment later, it was as though my vision was struck by a blaze of incredibly powerful light. In a split second, I somehow "heard" in my heart a voice say: "Hilary, I want you to follow me."

I felt a thrill in my heart, as though it was responding to its lifelong quest. Without hesitation, I climbed over the nearest five-bar gate, sat by the stone wall in that field, and said: "If that is you, Lord, I really want to follow you, but I don't know how."

I continued to sit, hardly daring to breathe. What was going to happen now? In fact, nothing happened and, after a while, I got up and carried on with my walk to Dalkeith.

When I arrived there, I looked around the shops, then turned around and walked back to Edinburgh. I kept expecting something to happen but didn't know what.

The next day, life carried on as normal. I still felt empty, cold and alone. Was there really a God? Perhaps I had imagined the whole thing; perhaps I was going loopy as a result of all the recent stress. Still, the hunger in my heart continued to grow. I really needed to find out if God was real.

The following Sunday, I set out to find a church. Surely this was where God lived and I would find him here.

I went along to the nearest church to the Royal Infirmary, which was in fact a Methodist Central Hall. It was a huge, dark and imposing building and I felt very frightened as I approached. A few elderly men and women were climbing the stairs ahead of me. I was beginning to think that this was a big mistake.

When the service began, I felt incredibly stupid. I was just one amongst twelve people in the congregation and their average age must have been 70 years. The service was dull and uninspiring and I didn't know any of the hymns. When the collection plate came around, I grudgingly put my two-pence piece on to it.

I couldn't wait for the service to end. It had all been a big mistake and I was trying to think of excuses for beating a hasty retreat. I hadn't thought that I might have to explain myself to anyone at the end of the service and had hoped that I would be able to leave, unnoticed.

However, just as I was leaving, a deaconess shook my hand warmly and began to ask me all sorts of questions. She seemed to be genuinely interested and she kept looking at me with what seemed to be piercing eyes. I felt very uncomfortable, but there was something about her that made me want to talk to her.

Deaconess Sarah Montagne invited me to tea the following Wednesday; she said that there would also be a friend of hers present. I hesitantly agreed to go, but as the day arrived, I kept thinking of reasons to cancel. Somehow, I did find her home and it turned out to be the most amazing "tea" of my life!

Sarah and her friend Fran were lovely to talk to. They listened and seemed to understand, and before long, I was telling them all about my search for God and about the incredible experience I had had on my walk. Very gently, they asked me if I would like them to pray with me. I had no idea what this would entail and part of me was frantic with fear. The other part was desperate to know if God was really there.

I did not realise it at the time, but the prayer continued for two hours. It seemed just a few moments to me. When

Sarah and Fran invited Jesus to make himself known to me, I saw before the darkness of my closed eyes what looked like an incredibly white figure, almost like a sword, which seemed to split the darkness. I opened my eyes, and Sarah and Fran were looking at me. I felt a strange warmth in my heart. Something had happened. It had really happened. I wanted to laugh, to cry, to hug them both, but with typical British reserve, I just said: "Thank you. Thank you so much."

As I left Sarah's home, I went down the dark staircase and out into the warm sunshine. With every step, I felt that my heart grew lighter. I noticed a lady shuffling down the street, with all of her wordly possessions carried in two plastic bags and, for the first time, I felt a compassion in my heart which was as unexpected as it was overwhelming.

Further down the street, I saw a cat (I have never liked cats) and I found that I was marvelling at its creation. I really felt that my eyes had suddenly been opened and that I was seeing my world in a totally new light. I had never expected this to happen and I didn't understand how it could have happened, but the miracle of it all was that it was happening. It was as though God was showing me his world from his perspective, and it was so different from the world I had seen before.

Back at the Infirmary, I met up with Shahida, a student nurse from Manchester, who was also a Christian. Shahida was small and effervescent, and was always smiling. Shahida invited me to attend the Hospital Christian Fellowship and, in spite of my feelings of inadequacy, she welcomed me into this fellowship where I felt nurtured and encouraged, and began to understand what being a disciple of Jesus really means. It remained a constant source of wonder to me that Jesus should die in my place upon the cross, just because he loved me.

I found that I had an inverted sense of unworthiness – that God wouldn't have gone to all this trouble if he had really known what I was like. This feeling of guilt and shame continued to block my understanding of the completely undeserved love of God which he offers to all people of all ages at all times.

Shahida invited me to attend her church, Charlotte Baptist Chapel, which was situated in the centre of Edinburgh. It was with a mixture of awe and fear that I entered this impressive building.

We climbed the stone staircase and walked through the swing doors which opened out on to a spacious balcony. There were already many people of all ages there, sitting and talking quietly amongst themselves. There was a hushed expectancy and a sense of calm which pervaded the entire building.

Beneath the balcony stood the raised pulpit in a central location. Upon it hung a beautiful royal blue cloth with a golden cross embroidered upon it.

As we sat down, a man went to the front of the church and introduced the community hymn-singing. I had no idea about the hymns, but the people around me were singing so loudly that it didn't matter. The building was filled with praise.

After 20 minutes or so of singing, we all sat down as the pastor stood to lead the service. As he read from the Bible, I found that, for the first time, it began to make some sense. Jesus had come to earth in order to die upon a cross as God's perfect Sacrifice, so that whoever asked for his forgiveness and turned away from doing the wrong things in their lives, would be forgiven and would receive eternal life. We could not attain this for ourselves, because of our fallen nature. No matter how hard we try to be good and to keep the rules, we still fall short of God's own holiness. We can only be his friend if we accept the gift of his Son.

This was all so new to me. Unlike many people who study Christianity in depth prior to making a Christian commitment, I had met with Jesus from a very ignorant point of view. I had been won over by Jesus himself and was now in the process of letting him be Lord in every area of my life.

It was not an easy path to follow. I had to admit that many of my strongly held views were not necessarily correct and that many of my attitudes were judgemental and highly critical of others. I had to apologise to the Lord for holding grudges against people, because when we hold unforgiveness in our hearts, it blocks the way for us to receive God's forgiveness. With this in mind, I continued my nurse training, with a new sense of purpose and with the reassurance that I had a Friend constantly at my side.

Back at work, there were also more challenges. In one of the small side wards there lay a lovely gentleman who was dying from lung cancer which had spread throughout his body. I was asked to care for him and to make him as comfortable as possible.

I carried out the basic hygiene care of Mr Murray, with as much gentleness as possible. He drifted in and out of consciousness throughout the morning. When he was conscious, he kept asking for a drink. I gave him sips of water, cradling his head in the crook of my arm. He said that his mouth was very dry, so I gently cleaned it with little foam sponges from an oral hygiene pack.

He was very pale and yet very jaundiced, as the metastases had spread to his liver. He was in a lot of pain and, throughout the morning, one of the staff nurses had administered pethidine repeatedly, in an attempt to keep his pain under control.

It was almost lunchtime and Mr Murray was again moaning in pain. Staff Nurse Butler took me aside. "Nurse McIntosh, would you like to give Mr Murray this injection? I must warn you, though, that it may well be the last injection he receives, as he could well die as a result of having too much pethidine in his system, because he has had so much already today."

I looked at her in horror. "No, no, thank you. I'm sorry, I know that he is in terrible pain and that he is going to die very soon, but I don't think that I can give this injection. Is that all right?"

"Yes, that's fine. I just wanted you to have the choice. Come with me anyway."

Together we checked the quantity of the drug to be administered and signed the controlled drugs book and then, with a heavy heart, we entered the little room once again.

Mrs Murray sat beside the bed, her lovely face stained with tears. Her husband was very pale and his skin was saturated with a fine sweat. Staff Nurse Butler explained to them both that she was giving the injection and then we quietly left the room.

Twenty minutes later, a weary and pale Mrs Murray came to the door of the room. Staff Nurse Butler put her arm around the older lady's shoulders. "Has he gone?" she asked quietly. Mrs Murray nodded; then sobs began to shake her shoulders and she gasped for breath.

We all went quietly into the little room where the still, pale figure lay, at peace at last. We all stood in silence for a few moments.

"You can stay with him for as long as you need to," the staff nurse explained to Mrs Murray. I was told to leave the room and, about an hour later, when the doctor had confirmed death, I was instructed to lay out the body, which I did, with a heavy heart.

The incident had raised issues of conscience for me. Was it right to leave someone dying in such pain, or was it right to ease their pain, but, in so doing, to speed the end of their life? It was a question that I have sought to come to terms with, to this very day.

Chapter Four

Following the eight weeks spent on this ward, it was time for us to return to a study block of four weeks' duration. This gave us all the opportunity to reflect upon our experiences thus far; it was becoming more and more apparent that there were some who were beginning to think that perhaps nursing was not the career for them.

I was hanging on grimly. I still suffered with a terrible lack of self-confidence and was far too sensitive to criticism. This four-week period did serve as a breathing space, however, and it gave us all a chance to regroup.

During this period, we were learning a little more about medical and surgical nursing, and we were visited by a hypnotherapist. The idea behind this visit, I believe, was to teach us just how susceptible people can become when they are in a vulnerable situation, for example, when they are a patient in hospital.

The hypnotherapist instructed the group to sit with our hands firmly clasped on our desks and then he instructed us to release our hands. Four or five girls found that they could not release their fingers, that they were stuck fast. The hypnotherapist gave an instruction, and the girls' hands were freed.

It was a puzzling and worrying thing to see these girls under the influence of someone they did not even know, and it made us all realise, a little more, how frightening it can be for patients to be under the direction of total strangers in hospital.

We had another visitation from a nutritionist, who said

that she was going to give one side of the room a pleasant solution to swallow, and the other group a very unpleasant one. We all responded in the expected manner – those who were told that the drink was pleasant enjoyed it, and the others said it was terrible. It was with a wry smile that our speaker informed us that they were both in fact the same solution! This taught us the power of persuasion.

All too soon, the study block, with its regular hours, came to an end and we were re-allocated to another ward. For me, this was to prove the epitome of my love-hate relationship with nursing, because it involved peripheral-vascular surgical nursing, which I loved, combined with the most spiteful bully of a ward sister I have ever had the misfortune to work with.

It bewildered me as to why Sister Dunblane was so vindictive. She was young, attractive, and ran an efficient ward on the upper floors of the hospital where the windows allowed in the sunshine. And yet, from my first meeting with her, I knew that she would attempt to make my eight-week allocation on her ward one of absolute hell.

"Nurse! Come here!"

The shift had begun only five minutes previously and I, the nameless, was summoned to her report. This was held in the entrance lobby to the Nightingale Ward; we were seated in a circle and questioned, without prior warning or experience, about various peripheral-vascular conditions.

More experienced members of staff smiled smugly as I attempted to answer Sister Dunblane's questions. It was humiliating and she knew it.

Eventually, her report and interrogation came to an end, and our work began. Within a few minutes, I was back where I belonged – attending to my patients. I loved the fact that all the theory was now becoming practice; all the anatomy and physiology we had so rigorously been learning seemed to be so relevant to this branch of surgical nursing.

I also enjoyed the sheer variety of work on this ward. It ranged from pre- and post-operative care of patients who had their varicose veins removed, to the near-intensive care of patients who had a graft inserted to repair a dissecting aortic aneurysm, and everything else in between these two extremes.

It was during this time that I was also beginning to come out of my own long, dark tunnel. I was beginning to make friends with other members of staff via the Hospital Christian Fellowship, and church was a haven for me.

One person in particular came to my rescue. Her name was Stella. Stella was a retired missionary who had been working in India for the previous 40 years and had dedicated her life to sharing her faith in Jesus with students.

Stella was introduced to me by Shahida; I was at once struck by the intensity of her gaze and the amazing energy and sense of urgency which pervaded her. She never seemed to appear tired and always had a diary full of engagements. For one in retirement, she made me wonder what she must have been like when she considered herself to be employed!

Upon retiring to Edinburgh some two years previously, Stella had formed a Christian support group for overseas students. She seemed to understand the terrible loneliness and isolation which many of these people experienced. It was strange, but I also seemed to fit into this category, for, although I had come home to Britain, Britain was not really my home. Stella seemed to understand this and she extended her warmth and care to me, for which I was so grateful.

One day at church, Stella said: "I need to come and speak with you about some Chinese students. Would it be OK if I came at about three o'clock?"

"Of course," I said. "I'll meet you at the main entrance to the nurses' home and show you to my room."

For some reason, I completely forgot that Stella was due to arrive. The next I knew of the meeting was a knock at my door, and there she stood. In a flat spin, I welcomed her in and offered her some tea. I rushed out of the nurses' home, ran to the little shop at the top of the hill to buy some biscuits, and dashed back with a teapot of tea, attempting not to appear too out of breath. Perhaps the running practice had come in handy after all.

Stella proceeded to talk about the Chinese students with great concern. Some were experiencing great hardship, trying to cope with the culture shock and weather, and with the isolation that many of them felt. As she talked, I began to feel that I was not alone in my struggles and that there were many others out there who were in the same predicament as myself.

Stella asked me to accompany her on a visit to some of these friends. I felt totally ill-equipped. What could I possibly have to say that would be of any benefit to anyone? I felt that all I wanted was for someone to come and take my pain away, but I had the uncomfortable feeling that God was doing the job his way and that this would involve growing beyond a place of feeling safe and cosy, and learning to serve others from a place of vulnerability.

Stella had recently acquired a blue Ford Viva which had come, as everything else in her life, as an answer to prayer. I found this totally amazing, that God should actually be able to provide for material needs as well as attend to those of the spirit.

It was with some alarm that we bunny-hopped down Lauriston Place outside the Infirmary. Stella assured me that this was owing more to the temperament of the car (which, incidentally, was called "Roo") than her own driving skill. We tore everywhere with characteristic verve and dynamism, dreading the change of traffic lights which would inaugurate another hopping fit for the poor car.

We drove through the city to the outskirts and parked

outside a block of flats. The lift, of course, was not working, so Stella and I climbed to the twelfth floor, stopping only momentarily on the ninth for us both to catch breath. Keeping up with this lady was proving to be quite a challenge.

We were welcomed into the flat with great warmth and affection, and invited to sit down and take a cup of tea. It seemed as though there were 20 or more Chinese students in the flat. I wondered how many of them were visitors and how many were actually sharing the sparse amenities.

I felt very awkward when I was offered one of only two chairs in the living room, but our hosts insisted upon this. In spite of their evident hardship and difficulties, they portrayed a deep sense of dignity and, upon their faces, combined with fatigue and suffering, was gentleness and peace. As they talked, the students were excited to tell Stella about answers to prayer that they had received and also of news back home, where some of their families had also come to trust Jesus as their Saviour and Lord.

It was not so for all; some of the students told of their worries concerning their studies and their families. It was literally tearing some apart to hear of news of mistreatment of loved ones back home, and some were not sure that they would be able to continue with their studies in Edinburgh because of this.

Stella seemed to know just what to say to each and every person present. She rejoiced with those who were buoyant and she comforted and supported those who were struggling. I watched in amazement.

As the time came for us to leave, Stella suggested that we all pray together. She led us in prayer, and a great sense of peace and hope came upon us. It really felt as though the Lord himself had visited us that afternoon. It was not false or forced; we had simply shared with each other the realities of life in a genuine and unpretentious way, and God had met with us.

As we bunny-hopped back to the nurses' home, Stella turned to me and said, "You are a brick, Hilary."

I wasn't quite sure what she meant.

Back on the ward, I continued to battle with the undermining comments of Sister Dunblane, who would one second order me to check the observations of temperature, pulse, respirations and blood pressure of a patient and then, 30 seconds later, call me away before giving me enough time to record my observations on the appropriate charts.

By now I was beginning to tire of this and would not come running to her until I had accurately recorded the observations. For this she would reprimand me. I was in a no-win situation. If I came running without recording the observations, then that would mean that the recordings would have to be taken again; if I did not come running immediately, she would accuse me of being slow and dilatory.

I decided that the care of my patients should come first and that checking and accurately recording observations should win the day. For this I was reported to my clinical nurse tutor who regularly came to teach practical nursing skills on the ward. I was very upset that Sister Dunblane should do this and I explained to my tutor what the situation was.

There was no noticeable improvement in Sister Dunblane's attitude and it made me wonder that such a case of outright bullying should be tolerated. Thankfully, after four weeks of day duty on the ward, I was then to commence four weeks of night duty, which meant that I would not have to work with her for the remainder of my time on the ward.

It's quite an experience preparing for night duty. You don't really know quite what to expect. There were all the rumours about how many people arrest during the night and how two o'clock in the morning is the time when most people die. Consequently, by the time I stepped on to the ward, I was already feeling extremely apprehensive. I needn't have been so afraid. The night staff nurses were lovely and I began to relax when allowed to do my job without being continuously harassed by Sister Dunblane.

The work was challenging and it was great to see nurses dealing with situations for which they would automatically refer to a doctor during the day. I was shown how to re-site intravenous infusions which had become blocked and how to check and give intravenous medication. Along with all the normal nursing duties, the nights passed rapidly. There was a real sense of being part of a team.

One night in particular was very memorable. It occurred towards the end of my placement. I came on duty and was told that I was to "special" a gentleman who was a bilateral amputee. He had undergone an aortic "Y" graft operation some two days previously and had been transferred from Intensive Care just two hours before.

Mr Shaw had several intravenous infusion lines in situ. He was catheterised and was also attached to a cardiac monitor. I felt rather overwhelmed as I entered the little side ward and was not sure that I would be competent to attend to all of these pieces of technology. At that time, intravenous infusions were not administered on the general wards via electronic counters, as they are today. Nurses were taught to count the flow of these fluids in drops per minute and constantly adjust the flow according to the patient's change of position. With several infusion fluids being administered simultaneously, it could be quite daunting.

However, the staff nurse who had been attending to Mr Shaw explained all that was necessary; I was all set to spend the night checking vital signs and recording fluid balances, and to be at the ready should any change in Mr Shaw's condition occur. At about ten o'clock, the senior house officer came in to visit his patient. He took one look at me, and the single blue line on my nurse's hat, and said: "Are you sure you're up to this job? Wouldn't you be better suited to sitting drinking tea and doing your knitting?"

I simply carried on with my observations and tried to put retaliatory thoughts out of my mind.

At about midnight, Mr Shaw's blood pressure dropped suddenly. I alerted the staff nurse in charge, and a senior house officer was called. Within a few minutes, Mr Shaw had arrested and the crash team were called. They managed to revive him and, by two o'clock, he was left in my sole charge again.

A couple of hours later, there were signs that Mr Shaw's level of consciousness was lightening. We called the anaesthetist who removed the endotracheal tube. An hour later, Mr Shaw opened his eyes.

"Where the heck am I?" were his first, very croaky, words.

"You're back on the ward after your operation," I said.

"Wha' the heck are all these wires 'n' things sticking in me for?" He was beginning to get quite agitated.

"These are all here to help you. They are giving you fluids and antibiotics, and other drugs to help you to recover."

"I don' wan' to recover! Don' yer see, I wanted to die! Wha' did yer have to keep me here for?"

What a question! I didn't know what to say. So I said the first thing that came into my mind.

"It's because you matter." A look of utter disbelief and disgust crossed Mr Shaw's face.

"How the heck can yer say that? I'm an alky and I've smoked both ma legs off. I canny do noth'n form'sel' no more. How can yer say that I matter? Yer must be chuffin' mad!"

I looked at him, struggling with the dilemma of his terrible distress and the very strong feeling that Jesus really loved this man, in spite of his own low opinion of himself. I did not want to force anything upon anyone, let alone my own spiritual convictions, but I could not let this moment pass.

"It's because Jesus loved you enough to die for you."

There was silence. Mr Shaw closed his eyes. I think that he could not believe that not only had he been resuscitated against his will, but he had also landed in the care of a Bible-basher.

For a couple of hours he slept and I continued with my observations. The first grey fingers of morning began to show themselves around the edges of the blind at the window.

I felt cold and tired. Mr Shaw woke. "You still 'ere?"

"Yes, I'm here."

"Thanks, hen."

Chapter Five

Shahida was rapidly becoming a close and very dear friend. She had the uncanny knack of always knowing how to cheer people up and we would spend many hours off duty just talking about life, work and faith, and usually end up in a fit of giggles about the absurdity of it all.

I felt very honoured to be considered her friend and, after five room changes within the nurses' home, brought about by insanitary conditions and the threat of collapse of some areas, Shahida and three other girls invited me to move out into a shared flat in Spottiswoode Street, just across the Meadows.

I was thrilled to be asked, and accepted eagerly. The move went smoothly enough and the five of us set up home with great enthusiasm. We hadn't anticipated a few practical pitfalls, however.

As winter approached once again, we would awaken to find ice not only on the outside of the windows, but well and truly encrusting the inner window frames as well! There was no central heating and the rooms had such high ceilings that they were always very cold indeed.

Then came the problem with the rota of sharing bedrooms. There were three bedrooms and five of us. Donna, the girl who insisted on the single room, refused to rotate to a shared room after the pre-arranged three-month period. This led to frustration and resentment amongst the rest of us.

Donna was experiencing real difficulties concerning her nursing career; we did not feel it was fair to put pressure on her to move out of her room, so the four of us agreed to rotate instead. I found myself sharing with a student nurse who was due to sit her final exams fairly soon. Her name was Debra and I was in awe of her.

Debra always seemed to be so serene and calm, and always walked and spoke with great poise and dignity. She was never flustered and was the leader of the Hospital Christian Fellowship. It was amazing how women like Shahida and Debra could cope with so much. I prayed that one day I would become like them. I'm still waiting for the answer to that one!

It was at this time that I decided I wanted to make a public affirmation of my faith. I felt bowled over by God's love for me and wanted to express this in a way that showed him that I was committed to following him. I therefore approached the elders of the Chapel and asked them if I could be baptised.

It so happened that they were about to begin a series of baptism preparation classes and so my name was added to the list. It felt strange to be interviewed by these experienced men of faith; I found it difficult to put into words the ways in which Jesus was beginning to change my life.

As the day of the baptism drew near, I felt that I really needed to give a mini-testimony at the service, explaining what Jesus meant to me. I was terrified. The Chapel can hold 1,000 people when full and the thought of standing up in front of so many made me very frightened. Even on the morning of the service, I still was not able to commit myself to saying anything. We were not pressurised to do so but gently persuaded that it would add extra meaning to the service for those who had come to watch.

We were given long white robes with leaded weights in the hems, so that the gowns did not bob up in the water when we walked down into the baptism pool. We were instructed that, when our name was called, we would need to walk forward, give our testimony, and then walk down the steps of the pool, where the pastor and one of the elders would already be standing.

We would then be asked three simple questions: "Do you believe in God the Father? Do you believe in God the Son? Do you believe in God the Holy Spirit?" We were to answer "I do" to each of these and then the pastor would say, "Upon your confession of faith, I now baptise you in the name of God the Father, Son and Holy Spirit."

With that, we would be tipped backwards into the water, so that we were totally submerged, and then helped up again. This symbolised our dying to the old life, before we had met with Jesus, and rising to the new life which he was now calling us to lead.

On the evening of the baptism, there were six very nervous candidates, all dressed in the gowns and feeling rather scared. The service commenced and we waited for our call to come forward. The Chapel was overflowing – many members of the congregation had brought friends along with them to see the baptisms. The air was thick with anticipation and, still, I was not sure if I would be able to give a testimony.

After the first hymn, the baptisms began and the first candidate was called forward. As he was lifted up from the water, the Chapel erupted with spontaneous applause, and a wave of encouraging support seemed to wash over us all.

The same thing happened with the next person, and then it was my turn. In my hand I was clutching a script which I had written and rewritten over again. My knees were knocking as I walked towards the microphone. I caught sight of Shahida's face beaming encouragement at me.

I stood next to the microphone; a little squeaky voice came from somewhere. "I would just like to say that Jesus has been changing my life so much. I was once very materialistic, but that is changing. In the words of the old hymn, 'Amazing grace', I once was lost, but now am found, and I really want to thank the Lord for that."

A lump came to my throat and I could no longer speak. I turned to the pool and walked slowly down into the warm, clear water. Standing there, answering the questions, I prayed that the Lord would know that I really loved him and that I wanted to know him more. Coming out of the water, I felt such joy. Jesus had died to save me from my sins and, in that moment, I felt that I had nailed my colours to the mast. I determined to follow the Lord wherever he chose to lead me.

After the service, people came forward to offer support and congratulations. I was elated. A wise lady stepped forward. "Well done, my dear; that was wonderful. Just be careful now, because very often after revealing your faith, there comes a time of trial."

I listened intently. "What do I need to do?"

"Just make sure that you keep your eyes on him and keep praising when the difficulties come."

"Thank you. I will try to do that."

With that, she squeezed my hand, smiled, and turned away.

A couple of days later, I commenced my second period of night duty, this time for eight weeks on Ward 27, Female Medical. Winter was well on its way again and Edinburgh was bracing itself against the harsh "lazy" wind which doesn't bother to go around – it just goes straight through you.

Night duty this time round promised to be all that I had feared. The ward was completely full. Instead of 30 patients, we routinely had 35 or 36. At one stage, the ward contained fifteen CVA (cerebrovascular accident), or stroke patients, who were totally disabled. Each required manual lifting and turning, and, very often, bed-changing every two hours.

Due to the inclement weather, we were always at least one member of staff down, and all the teaching about turning patients in their beds with two members of staff had to be modified to managing completely alone.

At some point in the night, there would be a visitation from the night nursing officer. She would expect the first-year student to take her on a tour of the ward and, without the aid of notes, to tell her the name, age, diagnosis and progress of each patient on the ward.

She would ask searching questions; it became increasingly difficult, as each night passed, to remember information from that night's report, as opposed to information from the previous night.

The night nursing officer seemed to move by stealth. She would appear out of the gloom and seemed to move almost silently. She could descend upon unsuspecting students with alarming results, but I was always so terrified as I anticipated her arrival, that she never quite managed to catch me out.

The combination of only three or four hours' sleep each day and an eight-night stretch of duty, each of twelve hours' duration, can cause havoc with the equilibrium. I well remember one night, when, having spent five hours solidly changing wet beds and attempting to settle very agitated ladies, I was given the opportunity to sit down and have a quick cup of tea.

No sooner had I sat down, than a very confused little lady started screaming for her mother. I went over to her and tried to comfort her. She settled down and I returned to my desperately awaited "cuppa". She same thing happened again. And again.

The staff nurse was busily writing up her observation charts and fluid balance and drugs charts, when Mrs McTaggart started to cry again. By this time, I was getting past the exhausted and into the hysterical stage, and started to crawl across the ward towards my patient. I was so tired and it all seemed so ridiculous. Staff Nurse McEwan began to giggle and so did the auxiliary nurse; the three of us giggled helplessly for a few minutes. Night duty can be like that.

The other awful aspect of working at night in the middle of winter was the fact that many patients did indeed die, and sometimes they were alone. For some, it was a peaceful passing-away during their sleep, but for others it was dramatic and terrifying.

One night, after completing the dreaded round with the night nursing officer, one of our patients started to complain of discomfort in her upper abdomen and back. Mrs Menzies was restless and distressed. I reported this to my staff nurse, who contacted the senior house officer on duty.

Mrs Menzies then went on to ask me for a cup of tea and, having checked that this was OK to be given, I headed for the ward kitchen to prepare this for her. Whilst there, I heard running down the corridor.

"Oh, no!" I thought. "What has happened now?"

I collected the cup of tea and walked briskly back to Mrs Menzies' bed. The curtains were pulled hurriedly around her and I heard the head of the bed being hastily removed. This is done in cases of cardiac arrest, so that an anaesthetist is able to insert an endotracheal tube for ventilation purposes. Surely, Mrs Menzies had not arrested! She had only just asked for a cup of tea.

With a sinking heart, I peered around the curtains and there, along with the senior house officer and staff nurse, stood the medical registrar, whose feet I had heard running only a few moments previously.

On the bed lay a prostrate Mrs Menzies. She seemed to be gasping horrifically – I had never seen or heard anything like it. And stranger still, none of the staff were doing anything at all, apart from standing and watching. Staff Nurse Browning beckoned me into the curtained area.

"What's happened?" I asked her. "Why isn't the crash team here? Why isn't anyone resuscitating Mrs Menzies?"

Jane Browning explained to me that Mrs Menzies, as well as having a heart condition, had an aortic aneurysm; it was this weakening of the major blood vessel in the body that was bringing about her death. The vessel had suddenly ruptured and this was causing massive internal bleeding. It was this that was making her diaphragm go into repeated spasms, causing the gasping and writhing.

There was nothing that anyone could do to help so, in the half-light, we stood and watched and waited. Each time the registrar thought that the end had come, and put a stethoscope to her patient's chest to confirm death, Mrs Menzies would gasp again. It was like something from a horror film and it is a memory that will stay with me always.

Eventually peace came. We were able to perform last offices and inform Mrs Menzies' relatives. It was difficult to bring comfort to these people, especially when they asked if she had had a peaceful and dignified death. Again, the phrase "The doctors have done all that they could" seemed to be the only thing that could be said.

As the first light of dawn began to peep around the blinds, and we busied with our observations and drugs rounds, I found it difficult to remove the images I had seen in the darkness from my mind. At the end of the shift, my hands were rubbed raw with the combination of urine and starch in the sheets which I had changed so many times during the night. I felt completely exhausted, physically and emotionally.

The following night, the eighth and final night on duty, we had a spate of deaths on the ward. It was becoming almost a matter of course to walk down the ward, and, upon finding a still, quiet figure in a bed, discover that the occupant had indeed passed away. The majority of the patients on the ward at that time were described as "not for resuscitation", owing to their condition and age.

Again, all the training about never moving a patient on one's own had to go by the wayside. There were just not enough staff on duty to cope with the workload, so I had to develop the skill of laying out patients single-handed, which I found not only very difficult from a practical point of view, but also very frightening.

Death seems such a strange thing. One moment, a person is considered alive; the next, they are dead. What concerned me was this: if they had only just died, were they still nearby? And if so, what could they do to me, the person who was attempting to prepare their body for the morticians?

Again, the lack of sleep, the exhaustion and the dark began to invoke a kind of irrational fear. It was a great struggle to keep this fear under control. I felt that if I didn't escape soon from the ward, with all its death and demands, then I would no longer be able to cope.

By the grace of God, the night came to an end. The relief of going home was immeasurable. I felt as though a cold greyness had taken over my entire being, and the fatigue was devastating. During the ensuing six days off duty, I would live in fear of the nights to come. I just couldn't bear the thought of having to return to such an ordeal for three more eight-night stretches of duty.

One phrase kept me going: "I can do all things through Christ who strengthens me" (Philippians 4:13).

I kept telling myself that this included facing up to the fears of the night and that I was not facing them alone. Fear is such a powerful emotion; it can totally dominate our attitudes and way of life, often with devastating results. When I read the Bible, it told me that God's love, perfect love, would drive out all fear (1 John 4:18). If I was going to trust him, then I was going to have to hold on to his promises.

Night after night, I faced up to my fears of death and the dark, and night after night, I was enabled to carry on and do my job. For me this was more than a tiny miracle – it was a major victory, by the grace of God.

Chapter Six

At the end of the eight weeks came the promise of a two-week holiday, for which I could hardly wait. My parents, still living in Hong Kong, had sent air tickets so that I could fly out to spend the holiday with them.

I flew down from Edinburgh to Heathrow and then caught the flight to Hong Kong. I had never flown alone previously and it felt very strange to be undertaking this journey, after all that had happened in the preceding year.

I felt as though I was returning to a former world, and a former life, to which I no longer belonged. As we approached Hong Kong's Kai Tak Airport, as it was then called, I held my breath as we seemed to skim the skyscrapers with the tips of the huge aircraft's wings. Having landed, it was wonderful to see my parents again.

Back at the flat, however, I felt ill at ease with the bedroom in which I had grown up. I felt that I had moved on, and that, in spite of all the hardships and struggles, the world I now lived in was of my own making; having met Jesus, life made a lot more sense than the world of luxury and high living which was Hong Kong.

The holiday was spent going out to various country clubs and, of course, to the stables for retired racehorses at Bees River. My father had a horse of his own stabled there and it was good to see her again. Having said that, she and I had never really hit it off. On the few occasions I had attempted to ride her, she had tried to take me off in completely the opposite direction to the one in which I intended to travel, and at a much faster pace!

Instead, Mum would ride Buntie, and I would run along behind. It seemed to be the most sensible compromise and, this way, we were all happy.

When the two weeks came to an end, I prepared to return to Edinburgh, only to have my flight delayed by twelve hours. This meant that I missed my connecting flight from Heathrow to Edinburgh and instead had to take a flight to Glasgow, arriving there in the middle of the night. With the help of a very kind couple of fellow travellers, I caught the train to Edinburgh and eventually took a taxi back to Spottiswoode Street.

Two days later, I resumed training. This was now our second year; during this time, we were to experience other areas of nursing. This would involve working in operating theatres, psychiatric units, obstetric units and the Accident and Emergency Department.

My first allocation was to a nearby psychiatric hospital which cared for people with both acute and chronic conditions. I was terrified. Following a very brief introductory course, I was allocated at first to a ward which cared for chronic psychiatric cases.

At once, I was struck by the thick, oppressive atmosphere of the ward. Almost all of the patients seemed to smoke incessantly and the staff seemed to do the same. The staff all wore casual clothes; sometimes it was difficult to distinguish patient from carer in such an environment.

The ward itself was dark and the few windows to the outside world were covered with what appeared to be decades of grime. The hospital seemed as a whole to be quietly deteriorating, whilst its inhabitants shuffled by, not noticing its demise.

Two days in particular stand out in my memories of this ward. The first occurred on one late shift, when the staff decided that I should accompany several patients on a trip to the pub. There was one other member of staff present and I found it quite amazing to watch the reactions on the faces of the other pub-goers as our patients indulged in some rather antisocial behaviour.

It made me realise how difficult it is for people with chronic mental illnesses to be accepted by society, and I felt ashamed that I also found the situation embarrassing and very uncomfortable.

The second incident occurred in my fourth and final week of placement on this particular ward. It was the early shift and I had been given some medication to administer to a gentleman in his 50s who was suffering from pre-senile dementia.

Mr Souter, as I will call him here, was a proud man; his bearing suggested that he had spent some of his life in the armed forces. He was tall and well-made, and his clothes were always clean and tidy. He was obviously a very articulate person, and his distress, caused by his condition, was at times overwhelming.

There were times when Mr Souter could recall events in his life with ease and then, suddenly, as though a switch had been flicked, he could remember very little. This brought about a sense of great disorientation and panic, and he felt very insecure and frightened.

On this particular morning, I had been told to administer Mr Souter's medication, but I was immediately aware of the anxiety this man was feeling. As I entered his room, he was pacing the floor and seemed very agitated. I felt frightened and made sure that I always had access to the door, in case of any sudden violence on his part. I offered the tablets to him, encouraged him to take them, and then left the room.

I reported to the staff nurse that my patient seemed very uneasy, and then was told to take another patient to the toilet. During this time, Mr Souter attacked one of the permanent members of staff. He had my colleague held in a commando-style stranglehold and had to be heavily sedated before he could be persuaded to release him.

It made me realise how vulnerable nurses are. We had not been instructed in any form of self-defence and we were really left to our own devices to cope with such incidents. It also made me very aware of the inadequacies of the system to care for such patients. Thankfully now, conditions seem to have improved markedly for those with mental health problems, but there is always room for further improvement and understanding.

The following week, I was allocated to an acute ward; this again was a totally new experience. Patients, or clients, as they were called on this ward, had been admitted following an acute exacerbation of a known condition, or had experienced their first episode of mental illness. This included adults who had been admitted following self-harming incidents or attempted suicide.

My first duty was to check the bathrooms for any sharp or possibly harmful objects, such as razor blades. I had to be on the lookout for dressing-gown ties, scissors, or any object which might possibly be used to cause harm.

I began to feel very anxious whenever I was asked to check the bathrooms and had visions of finding clients hanging from the rafters, dripping with blood. An overactive imagination is not always a good thing!

The majority of my time on this ward which, like the chronic psychiatric ward, would have had smoke detectors alarming continuously, involved learning to talk with people and to listen and observe what people were saying, both verbally and also through their body language. I found this fascinating. I feel that this was the most valuable skill that I began to develop during my time on this ward.

It was, however, not a place where one could just sit and chat. There were the weekly ward rounds, where each client would come into a room full of staff, sit down, and be interviewed by the consultant, whilst all the staff observed and listened.

It seemed a bizarre system and did not help each client to relax and speak freely, as it promoted a "them" and "us" mentality amongst the staff. I did not approve of this system, but felt powerless to do anything about it.

My other duties involved escorting clients to other areas of the hospital for blood tests, physiotherapy, electro-convulsive therapy, etc. Sometimes it was just necessary to escort a patient for a walk outside in the lovely grounds and, of course, this did not always go according to plan.

One day, I was sent out with a young lady called Sarah. She was almost exactly the same age as myself and had been diagnosed with schizophrenia; she was recovering from an acute episode of this. She was tall and slim, and when she was well, loved to take part in many sports. Sarah had asked if she could go into the main part of the hospital in order to buy some confectionery. I had said that this was fine, so we headed off down the main corridor.

As with many hospitals at that time, the main corridors were hundreds of yards long, with many doors heading off from either side. As we walked along, one of the doors was suddenly shut. I did not know that Sarah was terrified by the sound of a door shutting, but the next second, I found myself in hot pursuit of her down this never-ending corridor.

I am sure that the spectacle caused much amusement as Sarah and I flew along, but I was really worried about her, and did not know if, where, or when she was likely to stop.

As we neared the main entrance, I was hoping and praying that she would stop, but instead she hurdled a domestic's mop and bucket, and headed out into the sunshine. I had no option but to follow, so the pair of us ran straight out into the car park, where Sarah proceeded to vault over a parked car.

I managed to run around the other side of the car and to get in front of Sarah, and then try to calm her down. It's quite a feat when you are gasping for air and very unsure of what to say in the first place!

Thankfully, now that we were outside, the threat of hearing doors closing had diminished, and Sarah's fear began to subside. She gradually calmed down and we managed to return to the ward via an outside route.

When we got back, the staff looked quite amused. Evidently, news of our escapade had reached their ears and they found the entire incident very funny. I felt that this was, once again, another one of those moments that nurses very often put down to "good experience".

"I'm sorry I had you worried," Sarah continued once we were safely back in the ward. "I just can't stand it when I hear a door closing – I just have to run away. My mother cannae understand it either. I guess I'm a lost cause."

With this, she began to cry. I reassured her that she was not a lost cause, but in my mind I was thinking that she had very nearly been a lost patient.

Chapter Seven

As the next secondment loomed, I felt as though I was approaching it with a little more understanding and knowledge. The secondment to the psychiatric hospital had been difficult and sometimes harrowing, to say the least, but I felt that a lot of my fear of mental illness had been overcome by simply dealing with people who suffered in this way and by realising that they were just like anyone else who had a condition which required medical and nursing help.

I found my next placement to be in stark contrast. Having spent the last eight weeks learning intensively how to talk to and, more importantly, listen to my clients, my next patients were unable to speak at all – for the simple reason that they were anaesthetised!

Back at the Infirmary, I was seconded to one of the many General Surgery operating theatres.

This was a whole new world. Here, the surgeon was revered almost to the point of idolatry. We minions would all busy about, preparing the theatre with its multitude of trollies and surgical implements, diathermy machines and lights, and do all we could to assist his work as quickly, quietly and efficiently as possible.

The theatre itself was scrupulously clean, with pale green walls and large frosted windows which allowed as much light as possible into the working environment. It was the complete opposite of the world of the psychiatric wards, which had small, obliterated windows, and air so thick it could be cut with a knife. Here, the only thing that knives were cutting was human flesh.

Whereas hours had been spent in communication, now this was reduced to a few seconds of reassurance to the patient as the general anaesthetic took effect. It was strange – once this had been administered, it was almost as though the person on the trolley had given up their personhood. They were wheeled from the anaesthetic room, rapidly attached to the ventilator and various monitors, and then the surgical team set to.

The surgeons would quite often work in silence, which was only punctuated by the occasional quiet and quite disdainful word: "Cut", or "Suture", or "Specimen tray".

On my second day in theatre, I had been given the high honour of receiving the specimen for the tray. The only problem was that I was rather taken aback by the size and nature of the specimen which landed in it.

I suppose I should have been more alert, but when a very large piece of diseased colon was placed under my thinly veiled nose, it took me a while to decide what to do with it! The warmth and odour made me feel rather the worse for wear and I proceeded out of the theatre into the area set aside for the labelling of specimens, to try to clear my head.

Thankfully, one of the staff nurses came to help and we dispatched the specimen to Histology posthaste. The surgeon continued with his operation and the patient was returned to the ward to recover.

With the conclusion of the first case, the theatre was rapidly cleansed and prepared for the second. I did my best not to touch anything sterile and spent the remainder of the day hanging up blood-stained swabs on a rack, counting them with the scrub nurse, in the middle and at the end of each procedure. It was always a worry when a swab count did not tally; the surgeon would not close the patient until the count was correct. The missing swab was usually found at the surgeon's feet where he had discarded it.

I really missed the opportunity to talk with the patients and felt more at home in the recovery area where patients regained consciousness afterwards. At least here I could give reassurance and treat people as people, and not just a surgical procedure. The nurses who worked in theatre seemed to rather enjoy the lack of emotional outlay of such work and found their satisfaction in always being one step ahead of the surgeon with whom they were working. I guess it takes all sorts.

One day, I arrived for work to find that my theatre was overrun with surgeons and nurses who had been working through the night on a major case. A gentleman had a dissecting aortic aneurysm which had just begun to leak. Fortunately for him, the surgical team had arrived in time to operate; they were removing the weakened wall of the blood vessel and inserting a graft as a replacement.

I had never seen so many intravenous lines and so much blood being administered simultaneously. The atmosphere was tense, and the faces behind the masks were pale and drawn with concentration and fatigue. This was real-life high drama. This man's life was hanging in the balance, and the team of doctors and nurses were doing their utmost to save him.

It took a further three hours before he could be lifted from the operating table and taken, with an entourage of monitors, infusions and several doctors and nurses, up to the Intensive Care Unit. Clearing up after such a procedure was a mammoth task. It made me realise just how important blood donors are, for, without the generosity of many such people, this man would never have survived.

Later on that same day, a very large lady was due to have elective surgery for the removal of an ovarian cyst. As she lay on the table, her abdomen did indeed seem to be very distended. When the surgeon began the procedure, the reason for this immediately became very clear. This lady had an enormous cyst, easily as large as a football. The surgeon's face was a picture. The medical photographer was called and, having changed into "theatre blues", took several photos for the records.

Once the cyst was removed and the sutures were in place, this lady's abdomen had returned to a much more normal size. I am sure that she must have felt so much more comfortable as a result. At that time, there was no routine screening with ultrasound equipment, so it was sometimes a considerable surprise for the surgeon to find the contents of a patient's "innards"!

The four-week placement passed quickly. There followed one week of study, during which time we were prepared for our visit to the Simpson Memorial Maternity Pavilion, the very grand name of the obstetric wing of the hospital. It was situated on the sunny side of the Meadows and, here again, was an entirely new atmosphere.

I spent most of the four weeks on an antenatal ward, trying to decipher the abbreviated language of midwives. They kept insisting that "midwives are not just nurses; they are practitioners in their own right".

At report, I would sit bemused by the lingo: "Mrs Smith, 36 weeks, gravida four, came in with PET and small APH, possible placenta praevia. On bed rest [I understood that bit] for assessment today. Possible LSCS if condition worsens."

I looked at the midwives taking notes. They obviously knew what was meant, so I would follow their lead.

One thing that had been drummed into us during the induction week was the importance of observing patients who had PET (pre-eclamptic toxaemia). PET is a condition of pregnancy where there is a raising of blood pressure in the mother, swelling, or oedema, of her tissues, and protein in her urine. All these symptoms are brought about by the pregnancy. It is very important to observe for escalation of these symptoms because, should the blood pressure rise too high, the mother could have seizures which, in turn, could have devastating effects on the unborn child.

I consequently very diligently checked all the blood pressures on a very regular basis. The thought of finding a lady thrashing around on the floor, depriving herself and her baby of oxygen, was extremely worrying. Thankfully, that didn't happen.

On one of our study days, our clinical nurse tutor took us aside to show us the delights of the contents of several dozen specimen jars. Entombed in these, suspended in formalin, were the sad remains of many women's hopes and dreams. They were aborted fetuses of varying gestation, retained for educational purposes, with the mothers' consent.

As the jars were passed round, I could hardly bear to hold them. These little human beings seemed so tiny and complete and yet had never had the opportunity to see the light of day. I found it a profoundly moving experience and one which took some time to come to terms with. It seemed so wrong for life to be denied to these children, and I wrestled with this for some time.

The positive side of the experience, however, was that I could now visualise the fetus inside a woman's uterus at varying stages of gestation, and this was indeed very helpful.

We spent one week on the postnatal ward, helping to care for the ladies who had undergone Caesarean sections. In those days, it was not uncommon for women to remain in hospital for at least ten days post-operatively, which gave them the chance to recover from surgery and to have plenty of help with feeding their newborns.

Not many women were choosing to breastfeed at that time, so that gave us plenty of opportunities to feed the babies for the mothers. This was great for us because we could unlock our maternal feelings and thoroughly enjoy nursing these little ones.

We were not permitted, however, to witness the birth of any babies, which I think was a disappointment to us all.

We did, however, understand that privacy in childbirth should be every woman's right. Instead we had to make do with a rather graphic film, after which we had undying respect for all women who had ever borne children!

By the time our placement came to an end, I had begun to feel more at home in the realm of obstetrics. It fascinated me. The whole ethos of caring for women as they went through what must be one of the most miraculous events in any human being's life, never failed to amaze me. The physiology and psychology of it all held special appeal, as did the incredible privilege of nurturing new life. I was at last finding my niche, and knew that midwifery was a path that I would seek to follow, when the time came.

Chapter Eight

Not only were things progressing from a professional point of view, but socially, things were improving too. Life off duty still revolved around church and the Hospital Christian Fellowship, and I was beginning to feel that God and I were beginning to understand each other. Not that he had ever *not* understood; it was just that I didn't know how to hear him. On one particular day, however, this changed dramatically.

On this day, I had been busily preparing the flat for a visitor from a senior Hospital Christian Fellowship coordinator whom I had met at church the previous Sunday. Jackie had said that she would like to come and visit me, so that we could talk a little more about her work and she could explain the vision of the wider Fellowship.

I felt very nervous in anticipation of this visit and was regretting having agreed to it. As time passed, I found myself getting into a real stew. The flat was empty, as everyone else had either gone away for their days off, or was at work.

I frantically cleared each room, trying to ensure that the flat was presentable, and was almost at the point of crying with frustration, when a voice said, quite clearly, but firmly and gently, "Be still and know that I am God."

I spun around – the voice was as audible as yours or mine. I was shocked and frightened, but there was nobody there. I nearly dropped the tray I was carrying, and sat down. Could that be God? Was he really speaking to me?

"I'm sorry, Lord," I muttered. "Please help me not to get so agitated. I'm sorry that I didn't trust you."

A strange peace came over me – similar to the one experienced when I had gone for tea with the deaconess. A few minutes later, Jackie arrived and we had a lovely talk. I didn't dare mention the experience of the voice, because I thought that she would not understand and would perhaps accuse me of having an auditory hallucination of some kind.

In fact, I kept the experience a secret until the following Sunday, when the opening reading from the Bible was Psalm 46. When the pastor reached verse 10, which says, "Be still and know that I am God", I gasped. Shahida looked at me.

"Are you all right, Hilary?"

"I can't believe it," I whispered, "but I heard God say that to me on Wednesday."

"Oh, that's great," said Shahida. "It's wonderful to hear God's voice."

"I just didn't expect to hear him out loud!" I blurted.

Shahida gave me a searching look and then she said, "Well then, that was especially great!"

Back at the flat, all manner of interesting events were unfurling. Sophie, one of the student nurses who was a university graduate, was getting engaged; we were all very pleased for her. Donna was still enduring the training, but was looking for an alternative job elsewhere. She still hung on grimly to the single room.

Debra always seemed to be working, either on the wards or in the hospital library, and Shahida had taken over the leadership of the Hospital Christian Fellowship. We would quite often have the midweek meetings at the flat, and a wide cross-section of hospital staff would attend.

A very charming pharmacist had his eye on Shahida and, after a few weeks, summoned his courage and asked her out. Shahida said that she would prefer it if we went out as a group, so several of us went down to the city centre, to a health food restaurant known as Hendersons.

There they served the most wonderful array of vegetarian cuisine imaginable; the restaurant was usually very full. When we arrived, there was only one table available, so we placed our jackets on the chairs and went to the self-service counter.

When we returned to the table, I found that I was the last to be seated, so I took the remaining chair. A second later, I realised why it was the only chair left – it splintered to matchsticks the moment I sat down.

Finding myself viewing the table from an unexpected perspective, I heard everyone begin to laugh – in fact the entire population of the restaurant was laughing.

"Do you think that you should have gone for that helping of fruit salad?"

Amidst other such helpful comments, I tried to get to my feet with as much dignity as possible. It was pointless, though, and before I could stand up, I was giggling along with everyone else.

One young man, though, Derek, who worked as a porter in the hospital, was very concerned. Unfortunately, he could not see the funny side of the incident and he attempted to be extremely chivalrous. This just made the situation worse; I couldn't stop laughing. Eventually, though, order was restored and a replacement chair was found. I sat down very gingerly, amidst cheers from all and sundry, and then we carried on with our meal.

Derek continued to attend the meetings at the flat and I was beginning to get the distinct impression that he was very keen, and not only on the Fellowship.

On one particular evening, we were all sitting talking together, when Derek sidled over to my chair – he was sitting on a beanbag – and rested his arm on my leg. I didn't quite know what to do, so I tried to pretend that I hadn't noticed. I know that I was rather naive in the ways of the world, but this did seem rather too forward, from where I was sitting.

The arm remained resolutely on the leg; I was unable to move as it was only a very small armchair. I looked despairingly at Shahida and she looked at the arm, the leg, and then me, with a wry grin. I grimaced back, in a "Help!" kind of way.

"I think that we should have some coffee now," Shahida said, "Hil, would you like to help me?"

"Oh, yes!"

So the pair of us shot into the kitchen and prepared the coffee. The problem arose when we had to return. Derek was still on the beanbag although, thankfully, the arm had moved from the chair. Shahida and I served the coffee, and I sat down again. Before the arm could return, I placed the empty try on my lap and drank the coffee, looking resolutely ahead. I was hoping that this was giving the correct signal and that the message was being received and understood.

It was. Poor Derek looked very sheepish for a little while, and then recovered. He was only to be replaced by Jason, who was as round as Derek had been tall and lanky. Jason also had a very pronounced squint, which meant that I was never quite sure which eye I should be addressing when talking to him.

At the same time, a young man who was a friend of Sophie's fiancé came to the flat and asked if I would like to go out with him. All of a sudden there were men everywhere! I did agree to go out with Steve. We went to the ice rink and enjoyed a very funny evening, skating and eating pizza.

When the time came for him to leave, however, I found that I had a problem on my hands. I kept hinting that it was time for him to leave, but he took no notice at all. Ten o'clock came and, as I was due on duty at 7:30 the next morning, I felt that I needed to go to bed.

Eleven o'clock, and still the same problem. I made a hot water bottle and, cuddling it, said, "Good night, Steve, I need to go to bed now." His eyes lit up. "Alone."

He looked rather crestfallen at this, but picked up his coat and left.

Shahida had been in the living room and laughed when I recounted the story to her. "I wondered when you were going to get rid of him," she said. "With some blokes, you've just got to be very direct." I was learning.

Back at church, the age-old problem seemed to be unfolding in the Young Peoples' Fellowship. There was one young man who I thought was gorgeous. He was tallish and had the most lovely brown eyes and gentle sense of humour. I hoped desperately that he would notice me and ask me out.

One evening at a barn dance, Sandy did ask me to dance, but it was only one dance. A couple of weeks later, he fell in love with another girl and they were married within the year. It was so disappointing – I seemed to attract the oddest specimens of the male sex and yet be unable to gain the attention of the most desirable. I felt sad and miserable, and threw myself into the challenge of my next placement, which was Accident and Emergency.

This was the placement which filled me with the most dread. Here, I would be facing real-life drama, where every second would count to save lives. I was also frightened of what I would have to face here, in the forefront of nursing.

I was soon to realise all of these fears. On my first shift, a gentleman was admitted via a 999 ambulance. As soon as he was brought into the department, he suffered a cardiac arrest. All the staff seemed to know exactly what to do; it was like watching a colony of ants, each knowing its place and performing to a higher mind, as they attached leads to monitors, put up intravenous infusions, intubated, defibrillated, took blood, and pounded his chest.

The man was then attached to a ventilator, nicknamed "the thumper", which performed the cardiac massage automatically. This made a curious "bump, hiss" sound as it worked, which could be heard throughout the department.

I stood where I was told to stand and prayed for the man under all of the machines and equipment.

"Bump, hiss . . . bump, hiss . . . bump, hiss . . ."

"Pupils fixed and dilated." The anaesthetist seemed almost matter-of-fact. "Are we all agreed?"

To my dismay, all the staff nodded somberly. I wanted to say, "Please keep trying, just a bit longer! Please give him another chance!" But the machines were switched off, the thumper went silent, and the staff nurse turned to me and said, "Perform last offices, Nurse McIntosh."

The room emptied and here I was, alone again with a corpse.

Chapter Nine

Accident and Emergency proved to be all that I had envisaged; it was not long until I came face to face with all its extremes.

On one particular day, two young men walked into the department, both wearing baggy tartan trousers and sporting Mohican hairdos which had been dyed bright orange. I was asked to take a short history of their problem and it soon became apparent that they had been involved in a fight in the city centre and had each sustained minor lacerations from a broken glass bottle.

I cleaned up the wounds and then advised them both that they would need an anti-tetanus injection. One of the men said, "OK, hen, as long as y' dae it gently", while the other went the colour of a sheet. He began to tremble and then to sway, and I swiftly placed a chair under his sagging posterior. A cold sweat came over him and he began to cry.

"Are you all right? Do you need to lie down?" I asked him.

"No, it's OK, hen," said the other young man. "He's just afeart o' needles . . . You great pillock," he continued to his friend, "it's only a wee pinprick and then it will all be ower."

After a few moments of consideration, the colour returned to the sick man's face and he consented to the injection, although he did need to lie down for about half an hour afterwards in order to recover from the trauma.

The Mohicans had just left the department when two ambulances arrived, carrying the victims of a house fire. A family of four were admitted hastily and the smell of burning entered with them. Three of the family were shocked but had only minor injuries and mild smoke-inhalation. The fourth member was fighting for his life. He had been responsible for helping the others to escape from the inferno, and his breathing was seriously compromised as a result of his repeated exposure to the acrid smoke.

I was instructed to stay with the three patients who had sustained only minor injuries, whilst the senior staff attended to the father of the family. My three patients were strangely quiet and seemed almost unresponsive. They sat on the trollies, huddled in the blankets from the ambulance, staring into the distance.

I couldn't imagine the horrors that they had endured. And then one of the young women began to cry, quietly at first, and then, in great sobs, she began to release some of the fear she had suppressed at the time of the fire. The sound of her sobs seemed to awaken the other two family members and it was not long before they were huddled together, sobbing and wretched, as they relived the moments when their lives were literally reduced to ashes around them.

I felt inadequate to deal with their terror, but I did my best to comfort and to reassure them. I kept them updated on the father's progress. He was very ill, but his condition had stabilised, and he was being transferred to the Intensive Care Unit for observation.

Social workers arrived and arranged for emergency temporary accommodation for the family, who were then taken away to one of the wards for recuperation. Clothes were found for them all and counselling was arranged, to help them to recover from the terrible ordeal that had struck them so suddenly.

No sooner had the family been transferred, and I had cleaned and restocked the trollies, than a gentleman was admitted with chest pain. He was extremely large and filled the trolley to overflowing. I connected the appropriate chest electrodes to the cardiac monitor and administered the prescribed level of oxygen via a face mask. Mr Coulthard then said that he was feeling a bit better, and I was called away by Sister, to clear up some vomit from the corridor. The domestic staff were apparently on their tea break at the time and as the vomit constituted a health and safety hazard, being right in the middle of the corridor, I was despatched to deal with it.

With mop in one hand and bucket in the other, I set about my latest task. Around me, I could hear the sound of coughing and retching, sneezing and moaning, and the sound of the staff's voices as they communicated with their patients. All was hustle and bustle. The department's doors swung open, bringing in a blast of icy air as another ambulance brought yet more patients in for attention. Relatives were talking, some in raised, irritated tones, annoyed because they had been kept waiting. The receptionist's telephone seemed to be ringing incessantly.

And then there was the sound of the cardiac monitor. Above the clamour of other sounds came the steady "beep ... beep ... beep ... beep". I continued mopping and had nearly finished, when the "beep" seemed to become irregular. I rapidly put the mop and bucket out of harm's way and was rushing to Mr Coulthard's cubicle when the ominous "Beeeeeeeeeep" indicating possible cardiac arrest came to my ears.

Sister was one stride ahead of me. She flung the curtains aside, took one look at the prostrate Mr Coulthard, and lowered the head of the trolley, in what can only be described as a very practised manoeuvre.

A second later, the trolley was whisked into the resuscitation area and "the thumper" was back in business. I was told to go off duty as my shift should have finished half an hour previously.

As I walked sadly away, the receding sound of the thumper was ringing in my ears. It seemed to symbolise the department – cold, clinical and efficient, saving one life and then moving on to the next.

As I returned for my next duty the following day, the machine could be heard in full swing as soon as I passed through the rubber doors of the department. I felt myself lurch, and walked smartly into the wall. I still hadn't become accustomed to handling life and death in a detached manner. It upset me greatly to see the weeping and sometimes hysterical relatives, and I found it very difficult to cope with people who were dying before my very eyes.

To me, death seemed so final, so absolute, and yet I could not come to terms with the fact that a person's spirit could just disappear without trace. There had to be something more.

No sooner had I reported for duty than Sister directed me to one of the end cubicles and instructed me to lay out a middle-aged man who had been found dead on one of Edinburgh's back streets. He had no identification, nothing about him to help us contact relatives or friends, and here he was, dead on a hospital trolley, his only possessions the few stinking clothes in which he was dressed.

So, alone in the cubicle, I set about preparing his body with as much dignity and respect as possible. I gathered his clothes and placed them in a plastic bag, and then washed his body, placed a clean gown on him, and wrapped him in the mortuary shroud. I labelled his garments and his toe tag: "Unknown male – Accident and Emergency Department", and added the date and time of death, as certified by the doctor who had seen him.

The mortuary trolley then came and took him away. As he went, I felt overwhelmed with sadness. What a way to end a life, huddled in some back street, so poor and so alone.

But Edinburgh's streets were well populated with homeless people at that time. It was most unusual not to be asked for "the price o' a cup o' tea, hen" whenever I walked down to town. On one cold day, a woman came up to me asking for money; I asked her to wait a minute, whilst I went into a baked potato store and bought her a large potato with cheese and coleslaw filling. She almost threw it in my face. I don't think that her mind was really on food.

One Sunday evening, as I was walking to church, a middle-aged man, very shabbily dressed, came up to me and asked for the customary monetary handout. I told him that I was very sorry but had no money to give him. He asked me where I was going.

"I'm going to church," I replied.

"Can I come wi' you?"

I felt a sudden panic and, for a moment, my mind reeled. Would this man be accepted in a polite, decent congregation? What would people think if I brought this man into such a place?

Then I remembered all the teaching I had received about Jesus coming to meet with people such as this, and how he had said that he had come to reclaim the lost and the outcast. Who was I then, to stand in the way of all that Jesus had come to earth to do?

"Yes," I said. "Of course you can come with me."

His face lit up and together we walked to the church.

When we arrived, we were greeted by some very bemused faces. The usually bright Sunday smiles seemed to slip from the welcomers' faces. I took Bob by the elbow and guided him to a seat in the downstairs worship area. The community hymn-singing began and Bob was beginning to enjoy himself.

The people in the pew in front began to turn around and look rather panicky as Bob began to say "Hallelujah!" at the end of every hymn. I thought that his response was rather brilliant and wished that my British reserve could be loosened up enough to shout in such a way when we were worshipping a wonderful God.

However, it was deemed by the powers that be that Bob

was becoming a disruptive influence, so he was removed from the service before the pastor began his address. I sat in stunned silence as he was taken away. I wish that I had had the courage to make a stand on his behalf, but I was shocked and very upset. The address, funnily enough, was about welcoming the stranger amongst us. I wonder if anyone else found this at all hypocritical?

The following day, I wrote to the pastor and expressed my deep concerns regarding the treatment of Bob. He replied that he had to think of the welfare of the congregation as a whole and that one person should not be allowed to dominate the proceedings. From where I was sitting, Bob had just seemed to be enjoying worshipping God. That was surely nothing to be frowned upon.

I discussed the issue with my Christian friends; their responses were mixed. Some agreed with the pastor's point of view, and others agreed with me that we should not turn people away from church because they did not fit exactly into our "nice" Christian image. It makes me wonder how many people we have turned away from God by our attitudes. It was the first time that I had begun to think about church issues in an independent way and, like any adolescent process, it was painful.

A week of night duty in Accident and Emergency followed. During this time I was confronted by the abusive behaviour of multiple drunks and victims of overdoses. I was beginning to get good at dodging the vomit and wiping it up very quickly – it's amazing the life skills one develops as a student nurse!

Nail-trephining at two o'clock in the morning has to be one of my most memorable experiences. A lady had trapped her index finger under a filing cabinet earlier in the evening (I didn't find out exactly how) and her nail had become filled with blood from the damaged tissues beneath. The pressure which was building up was causing her a great deal of pain.

I was shown how to heat up a metal paper clip over a naked flame and then to press this into the nail, thus piercing it and releasing the blood underneath. I watched in gory awe as the staff nurse performed the procedure; the relief which crossed the patient's face as the blood came shooting several feet across the room was impressive.

One simple dressing later, the patient was ready to return home. She was so grateful, if somewhat taken aback by the method of her release!

From the sublime to the ridiculous: my next patient came through the Casualty doors, lying sideways on an ambulance trolley. For some reason, he had managed to lose a plastic cone up his rectum and had called an ambulance to help him.

The staff all looked at this young man in a very disapproving manner. I was simply bemused and wondered why anyone should want to put such an implement in such an inappropriate place. When I expressed this to one of the staff nurses, she looked at him and laughed. "Just think about it, Nurse McIntosh."

I thought about it but still was none the wiser.

Back at the flat, things were changing. Sophie's impending marriage and Donna's decision to leave nursing meant that the five of us would soon be separated. Debra was soon to become registered and was keen to return to the nurses' home. Shahida and I agreed to do the same.

It was with a mixture of sadness and relief that we left the flat in Spottiswoode Street. We had shared so many happy memories there and confronted many issues, grumbled over each other's use of the bathroom and washing machine, and quibbled about the phone bill. In spite of these things, I had been so grateful to be able to live away from the institutionalised atmosphere of the hospital for this year. I had learned so much from my friends as a result.

Now, however, it was time to return to the hospital. On a cold and blustery day, we packed up our belongings, hired a taxi, and moved back across the Meadows. Shahida and I were allocated rooms in the more modern part of the nurses' home. Shahida was on the fifth floor and I was on the second.

The room was fairly large, square, with enough room for a bed, desk and chair, and a wash-hand basin. The window looked out on to the rear of the hospital, where the porters trudged back and forth with trolley after trolley.

I unpacked my belongings, sat on the bed and, looking around me, thought, Well, here we go again.

Chapter Ten

Accident and Emergency had been an incredible experience and I felt that I had begun to come of age at last. It seemed easier to begin to use my own initiative and to handle people with more confidence than I had dared to before.

The first couple of months of my third year of training involved a placement to the Oral Surgery Department, which seemed a million miles from the intensity and variety of Casualty.

I was grateful to be given this placement because the unit was hidden away from the main corridors of the hospital and was a quiet backwater, where most of the surgery was elective; the ward therefore was much more predictable.

The staff there were, on the whole, much more relaxed, but there always has to be one, doesn't there?

This ward's particular "one" came in the shape of a very wealthy staff nurse who had married well and did not hesitate to flaunt this fact. Bejewelled and coiffured, Margery Frobisher would come on duty each morning (for she never deigned to work in the evening), looking the very image of a very well-known female politician.

As she took report from the night staff, Margery would play with the enormous engagement ring on her left hand and take out her nail file to complete the "bored housewife" image which she portrayed so well.

We would set to work – well, Margery would dictate, and I would run around preparing patients for theatre, receiving them back from theatre, and performing the post-operative care.

Most of the surgery was minor – removal of wisdom teeth being the most common procedure – but we would take care of all surgery pertaining to the mouth. This included the removal of oral carcinomas, which required special post-operative care and a lot of emotional support. In addition to this, we would care for patients who had sustained serious facial injuries as a result of road traffic accidents; this would involve "special care", where a patient was isolated and attended by a single nurse who was with the patient for the entire shift. This also involved care of the patient's other injuries at the same time.

These cases always worried me because, at the bedside, there was always a set of wire-cutters which the nurse was to use in case of obstruction to the patient's airway, caused by swelling or bleeding. Should this happen, the nurse would cut the wires which were holding the upper and lower jaws together, and thus help the patient to breathe again.

It always amazed me when patients returned to the ward a week or so later for follow-up – how different they looked when all the swelling and bruising around their faces had subsided. The human body is a wonderful thing and its ability to recover from such severe injuries never fails to amaze me.

One patient, however, remains forever in my memory because he was such a kind and gentle man. He had been re-admitted following a return of cancer to his tongue.

Angus was very frightened and upset, and had already had part of his tongue removed when the cancer first struck about a year previously. When he was admitted this time, he knew what to expect and was very worried that he would not be able to communicate at all, if any more of his tongue was removed this time.

In order to ascertain the extent of the size of this new tumour, Angus was sent off to the Radiology Department for some tests. A radio-opaque dye was given intravenously, which would show up on X-rays and reveal the size of the tumour and the blood supply surrounding it, and also any possible spread of the disease to the surrounding tissues.

Unfortunately for poor Angus, he reacted very badly to the dye and suffered a respiratory arrest whilst in the Radiology Department. Having been revived there, he was transferred to the Coronary Care Unit for 24 hours, to assess his condition. When I learned of his plight, I went up to CCU to visit him, as I thought that a familiar face might cheer him up.

When I walked into CCU, I was taken aback by the rows of monitors above the individual cubicles. There was so much machinery and it was very daunting. I was shown to Angus's cubicle and was shocked to see how pale and small he seemed in the bed, surrounded by equipment which bleeped and flashed in an alarming fashion.

Angus was pleased to have a visitor and his face brightened. We talked for a little while and I reassured him that he would soon be coming "home" to Oral Surgery. He seemed to be very relieved about that. His experience of the past 24 hours had been traumatic, to say the least. He said that he never wanted to have another X-ray as long as he lived!

The next day, Angus was back with us, but the news from the investigations was not good. He was told by the consultant that he would have to undergo major surgery and would lose almost all of the remainder of his tongue. The tumour had not spread to the lymph glands, however, so he would not have to undergo chemotherapy in an attempt to stop the cancer spreading any further. This was a great relief.

Angus was nevertheless thoroughly depressed at this news. For a couple of days, he refused his visitors. He didn't want to talk to anyone. He even talked of discharging himself from hospital and going and throwing himself off a bridge. All the staff spent time with him and we talked to him and listened as best we could.

The speech therapist came to visit him several times and reassured him that she would be able to help him communicate effectively, but Angus, who was only 31, found the situation extremely difficult and unfair.

On the day of his surgery, Angus had a group of nurses who were cheering him on his way and it fell to me to prepare him for theatre.

Angus was pale, he hadn't slept at all the night before, and his hands shook as I handed him his theatre gown.

"What's your first name, Nurse?"

"It's Hilary," I said.

"Hilary, that's a nice name. Thank you for helping me and for visiting me in CCU. I do hope that I'll still be able to say your name when all this is over."

The theatre trolley arrived and Angus was whisked away to one of the general theatres which had been booked to take this operation; it would probably last at least six hours. It was with a heavy heart that I made up his bed in a theatre pack and waited for his return.

Even Margery seemed concerned and kept looking at her diamond-studded wristwatch. The rest of the ward carried on as usual, with the daily doctors' round and the quiet reverential voices of the junior doctors and medical students. I pottered about absent-mindedly and kept myself busy talking to the other patients and attending to their needs.

At about three o'clock, we received news from the theatre that Angus's operation had been completed and that he was now being transferred to the Intensive Care Unit for observation following the surgery. His condition was stable and he had regained consciousness, but there was a distinct possibility that he could experience breathing difficulties as a result of the swelling caused by the operation in his mouth and throat.

I left duty with Angus very much on my mind. That evening, I attended a Hospital Christian Fellowship meeting and asked my friends to pray for him. It was not unusual for us to pray for specific patients and we ensured that we did not divulge unnecessary information nor breach patient confidentiality.

The following day, I was working an evening shift and I had hoped that Angus would have returned to Oral Surgery, but his condition had not improved sufficiently during the morning for this to happen. At about five o'clock, however, we received an urgent call from the Intensive Care Unit, saying that they really needed to free the bed for a patient who was even more seriously ill. I was delegated the task of escorting Angus back to Oral Surgery.

This involved a trip literally from one end of the hospital to the other, pushing an empty bed, with the help of one porter, along winding and undulating corridors, negotiating lifts and dodging visitors.

Upon arrival at Intensive Care, once again, I was taken aback by all the equipment and machinery which was at each bedside. A senior staff nurse gave me a brief résumé of Angus's care and showed that she was surprised that a junior nurse should have been given the task of escorting such an ill patient over such a large distance.

I explained that we were very short-staffed and that I was the only available pair of hands to do the job, and so, disapprovingly, she handed Angus over to my care.

The staff lifted Angus very carefully on to the ward bed and disconnected many of the leads and monitors from his body. Angus was still sedated and seemed almost oblivious to all that was going on around him. In many ways, I think that this was a blessing, as it must be extremely frightening to be surrounded by so much equipment.

One of the doctors came with us on the way back to Oral Surgery, for which I was very grateful. My greatest fear was of transferring a patient in a lift, and the lift getting stuck, or the patient arresting en route, as had happened to one of my colleagues very recently. In her case, she ended up astride the patient, performing external cardiac massage whilst the porter pushed the bed at record-breaking speed down the endless corridors!

Our journey went uneventfully and, apart from the statutory superior comments by the doctor that Oral Surgery was like going back in a time warp, we arrived safely. Angus was settled in one of the side wards and I was delighted to "special" him for the rest of the evening, while he slept.

The following day, Angus was awake and attempting to communicate. He had been advised not to try to talk, as his mouth and throat were still extremely raw. So he communicated in writing and, although this was frustrating, we managed. By the afternoon, he was able to sit out of bed for a little while, which improved his spirits markedly. He was fed via a naso-gastric tube for the first week.

A special liquid diet was then sent up from the kitchen and Angus went through all the emotions of a tetchy two-year-old concerning this. One moment he would say that he was starving, then, having commenced the meal, he would push it away in disgust and slump back in his chair.

We just had to be patient with him and encourage him that things would improve and that it was normal to experience anger and frustration after undergoing such traumatic surgery. Day by day, Angus improved. He began to come to terms with his liquid diet, his two-hourly postoperative mouthwashes, and a myriad of medication.

By the tenth day, Angus progressed from using the bedside commode to walking to and from the bathroom. This made his morale soar, and his old, familiar smile began to flicker across his strained face.

During the second week, Angus began to gain weight again. He had lost about fifteen pounds in weight and had begun to look very gaunt. This, together with a complexion starved of sunshine, had given him the appearance of an anaemic skeleton, so it was a considerable relief to all concerned when things began to improve. The speech therapy was also going well and Angus was able to begin to try and use his voice once again.

Initially, he sounded extremely husky and he found that his voice "wobbled" a great deal. This was because the muscles which are used in the production of speech had become weakened by lack of use. Angus had to perform specific exercises in order to help them regain their strength. It was heartening to go into his little side room and hear him practising away.

During the third post-operative week, Angus became confident enough to accept more visitors. A steady stream of well-wishers trekked to and from the side room, and his locker and shelves became overflowing with flowers, soft toys and sweets. Angus was always very generous with his gifts and shared them with the nursing and medical staff at every opportunity. His speech was improving, but it was still difficult at times to understand him fully. To facilitate this, Angus used pen and paper, and he was finding that he could now write much faster than ever! He had also had a crash course in sign language and we nurses were receiving quite an education in this as we cared for Angus.

A month after he had been admitted, Angus was ready to go home. He was excited and frightened at the same time. It was one thing to learn to communicate with nursing and medical staff who were aware of his surgery, but it was quite another to cope with people in the real world who were not necessarily going to be patient enough to try to understand him.

Support in the community was arranged via the district nurse and health visitor, and of course the family doctor. Family and friends rallied around and, on the day of his discharge, Angus was thrilled to be going home. As he left the ward, Angus turned to each of the nurses and gestured "Thank you" in British sign language. Walking out of the ward he turned back and, with a shy little wave, Angus signed "H I L A R Y", blew a kiss, and left to face the world again.

Chapter Eleven

Hospital and state final exams were looming large on my horizon. In Scotland, final examinations took place after only two-and-a-half years of training. This was then followed by two three-month placements of pre-registration.

In the run-up to the hospital finals, I was placed on a male medical ward for night duty. During this time, I would be in charge of a busy ward during the night and, at the same time, be attempting to study for the examinations which would decide my future career.

It seemed a tall order at the time and, in addition to this, I decided that it might be a good idea to learn how to drive. Shahida gave me the idea, as she had discovered a brilliant driving instructor who was blessed with a tremendous sense of humour.

During my first lesson, Eric explained the basic ABC of the pedals and went through the gear changes in the car whilst we were still stationary. He then let me loose on a very quiet road, where we achieved the dizzy heights of second gear, before stopping and turning around.

Unscathed, we returned to the nurses' home and I returned to my studies. The driving lessons took place twice a week and, after one month, during which time Eric chain-smoked and laughed through each lesson, he suggested that I should take my driving test.

"Hilary, you're a natural. You may have forgotten to turn left when I told you and it may have taken two attempts to reverse round that corner on the steep hill, but," he said, ever the optimist, "you didna hit anything. I'm sure you'll do just fine."

I, however, did not share Eric's confidence and contacted the driving test centre to postpone the test for another month, so that the final exams could at least be out of the way. There was also the small matter of "night duty in charge" to consider.

The prospect of this was filling me with dread. For the first time, I was solely responsible for all the nursing care given to each of the patients, as well as for completing the mountain of paperwork which was to be dealt with during each twelve-hour shift.

Drug rounds, which took about an hour at a time, were particularly worrying because there was no one else with whom to check the medication. During the drug round, a junior student nurse was responsible for all the observations. The nursing auxiliaries did a wonderful job of attending to the basic needs of the patients.

On one night, however, at about midnight, just as we had settled the patients, one gentleman asked for help to go to the toilet. Pat, one of the auxiliaries, took the patient and within a few seconds was calling for help.

"Nurse McIntosh! Mr Downey is feeling very faint. Can you help me to get him back to his bed?"

I dashed to the bathroom and, sure enough, Mr Downey was the colour of a sheet and barely conscious. I grabbed a wheelchair and together we managed to scoop our patient into it and then lift him back into his bed.

"His motions were very black," said Pat knowingly. This indicated the presence of blood in the motions. "And there was a fair bit of it."

"Did you flush it away, Pat?"

"No, and I've also kept a sample. It's on the shelf in the loo."

Pat was one of the rare breed of people who are blessed with an enormous amount of practical common sense, in addition to knowledge which had been acquired over years of working in hospital wards. Her very physical presence was one of warmth and geniality. She possessed the marvellous combination of a ready laugh, a smile that exuded kindness, and very broad shoulders, metaphorically speaking. She was an absolute gem.

"You're wonderful, Pat. Thank you."

I tested the sample and, sure enough, it contained a great deal of blood. The duty house officer was called and she attended the ward quickly. Together we put up an intravenous infusion of saline, and blood was taken for cross-matching, in case we should need to give Mr Downey a blood transfusion.

Meanwhile, his condition was still giving us cause for concern. He was still the colour of a sheet and still feeling very light-headed whenever he tried to sit up. His blood pressure was very low, with a systolic reading of 90, and his pulse rate was steadily increasing and was now about 100 beats per minute. Both of these signs suggested that he was continuing to lose blood. His heart was beating faster in order to maintain blood supply to the essential areas of his body.

To aid this, we increased the speed with which the intravenous infusion was running and, eventually, Mr Downey's condition seemed to stabilise. Satisfied that all was under control, the doctor left us in order to try and get some sleep.

An hour or so later, however, Mr Downey asked to go to the toilet again. This time, we took a commode to the bedside and, once again, he passed a large quantity of old blood, approximately 300 millilitres.

We fast-bleeped the duty house officer who contacted the surgical registrar. Before any more time was lost, Mr Downey was transferred to theatre where part of his ulcerated bowel was removed.

It had been touch-and-go and I was so thankful that we had been able to help this man. It frightened me that a person could lose so much blood so quickly.

Before we knew it, the first rays of dawn were creeping around the windows again. I was desperately behind schedule with the reports, fluid balance charts and observation charts.

I whisked down the ward with the drugs trolley, and bleary-eyed patients dutifully accepted their medication. Near the bottom of the ward, however, there were several confused gentlemen. As I approached their area, the pungent smell of faeces hit me most powerfully.

I looked beyond the curtains and there was Gerry, sitting on his bed, resplendent in his nakedness and eating his own faeces. That which he did not choose to consume he was wiping on the locker, curtains and wall.

"Pat!" I called wearily. "Could you please come and help down here?"

Pat could see by the look on my face that the forthcoming duty was not going to be a pleasant one. Taking one look, she went to collect a basin of warm water and a whole new set of bedding and pyjamas. Within about ten minutes, the confused Gerry was looking the very picture of cleanliness and, apart from suffering the odd curse and threat which had been hurled in her direction, Pat re-emerged from the curtains looking remarkably unruffled.

I staggered home from work that morning, feeling as grey as the dawn light. The pressure of night duty, lack of sleep, and the huge tomes of nursing revision which awaited me at home all seemed to conspire. I felt cold and wretched and, watching the sun rise, wondered what a girl like me was doing in a place like this.

I managed to sleep for about four hours, which was pretty good going for night duty, and set about studying for a further three. I decided that some fresh air might just blast the cobwebs away and so took a walk out to Arthur's Seat. Climbing the hill, I stopped repeatedly to marvel at the beautiful view of Edinburgh and its surroundings. The air was clear and the sun drenched all the verdant folds of the Seat with a soft emerald hue. It was beautiful.

I sat down, and the warm air yielded the gloriously moist aroma of sun-drenched earth. It was this fragrance that I had missed more than any when I lived in Hong Kong and I breathed it in gratefully now. Now I was home, amongst my own people, and trying my hardest to follow the course which was laid out before me. I felt that, if I just kept going, then I would make it. I was nearly there and I kept repeating to myself: "I can do all things through Christ who strengthens me."

The warm breeze and the soaring birds refreshed and revived my weary spirits. I walked home, grateful for the opportunity to come to such a lovely place. As I prepared for work, I knew that it would be extremely busy, as tonight was when we were due to be "on take", which meant that we would be the first ward taking admissions directly from Casualty.

As I walked on to the ward, my heart was in my throat, and my spirits sank to my shoes. There had already been four new admissions just prior to the night shift commencing. Following report, I had to finish the admission procedures and observations for all of these patients, in addition to all the usual duties. Having just managed to settle all the patients and administer the appropriate care to the new admissions, I turned off the main ward light and set about the paperwork.

The next sound I heard was the far door of the ward swinging open and the sound of chattering porters, and then the rumble of rubber wheels proceeded down the corridor. This was followed by another, and another, as, in true bus-like collectiveness, three new patients descended upon us.

Not only this, but, behind the third trolley came the Woman of Stealth herself, the night nursing officer. I stood in the middle of the first bay and, rather like a policewoman directing errant traffic, shepherded the trollies to awaiting beds. I smiled weakly to the nursing officer, whose eyes held more than a hint of amusement but whose mouth remained in a perfectly straight line.

"Good evening, Nurse McIntosh."

Is it? I thought. "Good evening," I said. "Would you mind if I settle these patients prior to taking you on the ward round this evening, as you can see that they have only just arrived?"

"Very well," she said. "I can see that you have your hands full."

With that, she turned on her heel and left the ward. I heaved a huge sigh of relief and began the task of admitting the new arrivals and sorting out their belongings and relatives.

It was about two o'clock before all was settled on the ward. The duty house officer had completed all of her duties and had gone to bed. Gerry was even sleeping peacefully. All seemed to be going well.

Pat headed for the kitchen and returned with a large pot of tea (known in the business by the pseudonym of "Mrs Brown") and a plate piled high with toast. The woman was hovering close to sainthood as far as I could see.

I carried on with the paperwork and with preparing the drugs trolley. As I stood up, the floor seemed to sway and I lurched forward, knocking one of the drugs charts noisily on to the floor.

"Are you OK?" It was Pat's caring voice behind me.

"Yes, I'm all right. I'm sorry that I made such a racket. I hope I haven't woken the entire ward."

I sat down again; the charts and reports seemed to swim before my eyes. I was beyond tiredness, and a cold grey weariness seemed to overwhelm me. I wanted to cry. It was suddenly all too much. All the studying, lack of sleep, and horrendously long hours were taking their toll. I grimly hung on to my promised verse: "I can do all things through Christ who strengthens me."

84

My inner heart was crying back, "Please strengthen me now, because I can't do this any more, unless you make it possible."

The night wore on. Mercifully the nursing officer did not return and the patients were remarkably well-behaved. The morning drugs round came and went. All the observations were normal and all was peaceful as the morning shift arrived. I handed over the report and struggled to make myself coherent. Feeling demoralised and exhausted, I left the ward and staggered home to bed.

Back in the nurses' home, one of my neighbours was embarking upon a marathon orgy, if the sounds coming from her room were to be believed. I groaned as I shut my curtains, and peeled off the blue uniform and slung it on the floor. I hunted high and low for the earplugs which were supposed to keep out all sound, and fell into bed.

Three hours later, I awoke from a dreadfully realistic dream in which a patient was dying in front of my very eyes and I couldn't remember the correct sequence of events in order to begin resuscitation. The dream had given me such a start, and my heart was hammering in my chest so much, that the chances of returning to sleep were nil. Outside, the sun was shining again and, in spite of the earplugs, I could hear all the usual sounds of hustle and bustle, of trollies transporting supplies and people, of the voices of the porters raised in salute and irritation. The endless trundle of ambulances back and forth, and the occasional siren moving at speed before turning in to Casualty at the last second . . . these were the sounds of everyday hospital life.

I turned over in my bed and began to wonder if there really was life outside all of this. The past two-and-a-half years had been totally devoted to the pursuit of this nursing qualification. It had taken every ounce of my strength and resolve to get this far, and now, on the very threshold of achieving my goal, I felt too exhausted to go on.

I climbed out of bed and knelt down to pray. "Lord, please help me. I feel so weak and I don't know if I can see this thing through. What am I supposed to do?"

In the silence that followed, a thought came to me that I should have a look in the Bible at the book of Jeremiah, chapter 29, verse 11: "For I know the plans I have for you . . . plans to prosper you and not to harm you, plans to give you hope and a future." I knelt and wept until the counterpane was sodden with tears. Then, as I cried, I became aware of a strong breeze in the room itself.

Its presence frightened me, because it was not the familiar Presence of the Holy Spirit. I began to pray more earnestly, "Lord, I don't know what this is! Please help me!" The posters on the wall, which all portrayed helpful and inspirational verses, began to fall. I felt as though I was in the middle of a spiritual tornado. I was terrified and did not dare to open my eyes for fear of what I might see. I knelt and continued to pray for God's victory over this thing, whatever it was.

I prayed on and, gradually, the breeze abated. The window wasn't even open and this phenomenon could not be explained by me. Peace came at last and I dared to open my eyes; several posters lay on the floor and the bed. In a mood of defiance, I pinned them back where they had been before.

Shaken, I hastily dressed and went in search of Shahida, to ask for her advice and prayers.

Shahida, as ever, was calm and knowledgeable. We prayed together and then we decided to go out to Hendersons for a treat. The food was wonderful and we went to watch the film *Gandhi*, as we were both off duty for the evening.

The film was inspiring. It really spoke to me of the need to persevere, against all the odds and difficulties put in our paths. I was moved to tears by the cruelty and the struggle of it all. That love could overcome such evil and opposition was indeed wonderful.

We walked home together and, once again, Shahida's uncanny gift of cheering and encouraging had done the trick. By the time we arrived back, we were both laughing again and the darkness of the previous night seemed to have vanished far away.

Chapter Twelve

The month of night duty was drawing to an end. On my final night, I was summoned to appear before the night nursing officer at 2 a.m. in order to receive an assessment of my performance. If I had not performed to a satisfactory standard, then I would not be allowed to sit the final exams and could be removed from the training altogether. I felt that, once again, I was on a date with destiny.

It felt strange to be walking the long, chequered corridors alone in the middle of the night. As I passed several wards, I could hear the bustle of the auxiliaries in the ward kitchens and the clatter of kettles on the cookers, as pots of tea were made for weary nurses and restless patients. The aroma of toast, and the half-light of the ward corridors, all portrayed a softer atmosphere. It was almost soporific. The mortuary trolley rumbled past on its sombre way and an insistent "bleep" preceded a fleet-footed house officer as he sped on his way to answer an urgent call.

I walked apprehensively on, past the X-ray Department and up the stairs into the Nursing Administration Block, where I had attended my interview, seemingly a lifetime ago. As I approached the large wooden door, I felt in awe of the centuries of history of this place. Generations of nurses had passed this way and now I was here.

The time on my fob-watch showed 1:59 a.m. I stood by the large door and waited for the last minute to elapse. My palms were moist and I could feel the familiar constriction in my throat as my heart thudded. What if I was told that I had not been good enough? After all this effort, I could not bear the thought of being told that it had all been in vain. Not only would I be without a job, but I would also be homeless. The thought sent shivers down my spine.

The second hand passed the twelve and, taking a deep breath, I knocked on the door.

"Enter!"

Walking into the office, I straightened my uniform for the hundredth time.

"Ah, Nurse McIntosh." The sharp eyes shone out above the steel-rimmed spectacles. "Please sit down." I sat on the edge of the uncomfortable chair. "How do you think that this last month has gone?"

Oh no, I thought. She's going to tell me that it's been a disaster.

I spoke up. "I think, well, I hope that it has been OK," I stammered.

"Do you like night duty?"

"I would not say that it is my favourite time of day to work," I replied.

"And why is that?"

The time for telling the truth was at hand. "I find it very difficult to sleep during the day, and the shift is extremely long."

Again the eyes peered out searchingly. Papers were shuffled on the desk and some were passed to me to read. "Take a look at these and, when you have read them, please sign them."

I read the assessment in disbelief. It was better than I could have dreamt. I read and reread several areas, and looked up at the figure watching from the other side of the desk. To my amazement, there was a smile on the face of the woman I had feared for the past couple of years.

"Well done," she said. "You have handled a full and busy ward very well and we are very pleased with your progress."

"Thank you, oh, thank you so very much!" At that moment, I could have hugged her!

"You don't need to thank me, Nurse. It is you who have done the work and you have done it very well."

I was almost ecstatic, and the control and reserve of the past two-and-a-half years threatened to give way to hysteria. "I was so worried when you came to the ward when we were on take. I didn't know what you would think – I couldn't believe that three patients would arrive simultaneously."

A knowing look came from across the desk. I suddenly began to understand that perhaps certain events were more than coincidental.

"We needed to know that you would be able to cope in such a circumstance. In nursing, always expect the unexpected."

Signing the assessment, I was dismissed, and floated back to the ward. I was so relieved and wouldn't have minded anything happening that night. As it was, all was well and, as the daylight came, shortly followed by the morning shift, the ward was shipshape, fine and dandy. I almost skipped home, my heart feeling lighter than it had for months.

Two days later came the first of the hospital final exams. As our set gathered in the examination room, I was amazed to see the changes in the young women who had embarked upon this adventure two-and-a-half years ago.

The years had taken from us the naive desire to simply help people who were in need. In its place had come knowledge and practical skills which held us on the brink of assuming responsibility for many people's lives.

The summer sunshine seemed to cheer us on as the papers were handed out. Taking a deep breath, I began to read the first question: anatomy and physiology – great – one of my favourite subjects. As I began to write, the tension and the fear began to ease away and the three-hour paper seemed to pass much more quickly than I had expected.

At the end, we were all tired and drained, and we gathered our pens and belongings and headed out into the glorious summer day. I went back to my room and lay on my bed, my mind reeling with all the information I had tried to convey over the past three hours. Tomorrow would come the second paper and, a few days later, we would be given our results, prior to sitting the state final exams the next week.

I felt restless and decided to walk out to Blackford Hill, several miles from the Infirmary and far away from the hustle and bustle all around me. As the surroundings became more rural and the fields were filled with sheep, my mind easily returned to the thought of Christ the Good Shepherd. I remembered the day when the prancing lambs had caused me to reach out to him in the first place.

I thought of all that had happened since then: the moments of sheer terror when confronted with dire circumstances for which I did not have the experience or knowledge to cope alone; the moments of joy when someone really appreciated the care given; the hilarious moments when faced with a confused patient streaking down the ward, making a bid for freedom and followed closely by a senior house officer bearing a syringe full of largactil to try to calm him down.

It was true – there really could be nothing to compare with nursing. As I climbed the familiar hill and looked out upon Edinburgh, nestled warmly beneath Arthur's Seat, I prayed that the Lord would help me to complete the task before me and that he would show me the way.

Sitting amongst the heather and the gorse bushes, I watched the birds soaring on the thermals above the hill. They were so free and the thought struck me that God was their Provider; I prayed that he would be mine also. The Bible tells us that God will never leave us nor forsake us, and I was holding on to this promise for all I was worth.

Coming down the steep slopes, many ideas were stirring – for the first time I began to think about life after the training. What was I going to do, always supposing that I was successful? It had always been my ambition to obtain the cherished "Pelican" badge, given to nurses who had trained at the Infirmary and had stayed on for a year afterwards as a staff nurse.

That badge symbolised so much to me: the sacrifice of always caring, always persevering, even when bullied and ridiculed publicly for doing so; the sacrifice of two student nurses lifting 220-pound men into and out of baths for three hours solidly each morning shift, without the aid of mechanical hoists; the effort of always performing to the best of your ability, even when frightened and over-whelmed; dealing with aggressive and abusive patients and relatives – being sworn at, but still having to maintain a professional and objective demeanour. These were the things which made the Pelican so appropriate, together with its rather comical appearance which seemed to embody the very bizarre events which could take place in the course of life on the wards.

Walking home, I decided that I was going to do all in my power to reach this goal. I spent a couple of hours studying that evening, before falling into a deep and restful sleep. Restful, that is, before being woken at 3 a.m. by the sound of hammering on my door as Linda, one of the girls on the second floor, ran shouting down the corridor, "Fire! Fire! Everybody get up! Get up!"

Like everyone else, I fell out of bed, grabbed my dressing gown, and headed for the exit. We all gathered in the des-ignated waiting area and a roll call took place. Some very sheepish faces appeared – more than expected – as scantily clad young men appeared, hiding behind equally scantily clad young women. At that time, it was a female nurses' home, so these guys felt rather conspicuous. The rest of us just groaned and wondered where the fire was and whether we were about to become homeless.

As we had rushed down the stairs, the air had been filled with smoke, in spite of the fire doors along the corridors.

The fire service arrived quickly and, about 20 minutes later, we were told that it was safe to return to our rooms. The fire had been in the kitchen, as someone had forgotten to turn off the cooker and had placed an empty saucepan on top of one of the electric rings.

As we climbed the stairs again, the acrid fumes made us shiver. It was only now that the danger of the situation seemed to strike. I climbed back into bed and found it difficult to fall back to sleep. All along the corridor, doors were opening and shutting as nurses talked about the incident and speculated about who had caused the fire in the first place.

At about four o'clock I went to the bathroom and, on my return, saw a shadowy figure through the fire doors at the opposite end of the corridor, where the senior nursing staff had their quarters. I wondered if this could be the newly appointed nursing officer who, Shahida had been told, was a Christian.

Trying to forget all the excitement and desperately attempting to restore the failing brain cells, I lay down again and practised relaxation techniques, breathing in . . . two . . . three . . . four . . . out . . . two . . . three . . . four . . . The next thing I heard was the alarm clock, and the memory that this was the day of the second hospital paper dawned upon my butterflies with great speed. They were off and flapping before my feet touched the floor.

The second paper was mainly surgical questions and this was OK. By the time it was over, all of us who had been disturbed during the preceding night were completely shattered. We gave the paper a suitably morbid post-mortem and then went our separate ways.

It was another couple of days before we would receive our results, so I decided to try to relax but still spend some time studying for the state finals, which were to take place in the following week. I took advantage of Edinburgh's Commonwealth Swimming Pool and enjoyed swimming length after length in the warm water.

An evening spent with friends from the Hospital Christian Fellowship helped to steady the nerves, as did writing home and receiving letters from home. Sometimes the post from Hong Kong would be delayed and I would receive two or three letters at a time.

The day of the results arrived and again our set gathered to hear our fate. Out of the 25 of us who were still on the course, 23 had passed. We were overjoyed, but very sad for the two who had received the bad news. They would be given a chance to resit the paper in the following two days and, if they were successful, they would have the opportunity to sit the state exams along with rest of us.

They managed to pass and, on the following week, we were all together again, sweaty palms and nervous laughs included, waiting in the corridors of the college, prepared to take on the examiners one more time.

The day was dull and uninspiring and, as we sat down preparing to receive the first paper, I felt tired and jaded. The adrenalin seemed to be running out and suddenly it all seemed too much once again. I closed my eyes and asked the Lord for help – it was only going to be by his grace that I was ever going to get through this.

Looking up, I saw the paper was placed on the desk. It is a terrible thing that a few sheets of paper can cause one so much fear. Taking a deep breath, I turned the paper over and, to my horror, the first question was on renal medicine. For some reason, the kidney had been the cause of a mental block for me all through the training. Its complex structure and associated adrenal gland secretions always seemed to outwit me.

I tried to say calm and decided to move on to the second question in order to get into the flow. The second question was all about the eye – another one of my weak areas. I answered the question as well as possible and then returned to the first. Suddenly, the mental block seemed to leave my befuddled mind, and the answer to the question came to me. All the confusing hormones and anatomy of the kidney seemed suddenly to make perfect sense.

"Thank you, Lord," I muttered under my breath and, with that, I was on my way.

The rest of the paper was a blur, but I carried on writing until we were told to stop. I hoped and prayed that it would be good enough, but only time would tell. Afterwards, the faces of my peers told a similar story. Each and every one of them looked pale and drawn. We all agreed that it had been much more difficult than the hospital exams; we were beginning to panic and to think that perhaps our tutors had not adequately prepared us for this.

Dispirited and upset, we all went home to indulge in one last night of revision. Some of the girls decided that they would go out and drink themselves silly, in order to forget the day's events. Others decided that an early night would help them feel better. I didn't want to talk to anyone and, as I shut the bedroom door, the tears began to fall.

Chapter Thirteen

The night which followed was not interrupted by fire, tempest or flood, but by an awful recognition that, somewhere along the line, I might have misread the question on cardiac medicine and given a completely erroneous answer.

The sane voice kept saying, "Don't worry about this now. There is nothing you can do to change the situation with yesterday's paper. What you need do is relax, so that you can do better today."

"Today! Oh God!" This was the panicky voice now. "You've got to do it all again! Another three-hour paper! Suppose you don't know the answer to any of the questions – what will you do then?"

"I'll just have to resit the exam, that's all. Now shut up and go to sleep."

I liked the sane voice and held on to its every word. The relaxation techniques came back into operation and, after another few minutes, the nightmare loosened its grip and I fell asleep once again.

The morning dawned grey and foreboding. I sat and watched an angry sky. As the sun rose, streaks of red flooded the horizon, and high-banked anvil clouds processed with grim determination. On the desk in front of me were files of notes and numerous revision cards, all to do with surgical nursing. Going to the kitchen to make some breakfast, I found once again that my carton of milk had been stolen from the communal fridge. I made porridge with hot water and returned to my room. I felt like a lifer on death row, eating their last meal before their fate is sealed.

A quick bath, some stretching exercises, and a few minutes of "Help!" prayers later, my feet were taking me back to the college to sit the second paper. Gone were the nervous, chattering girls of two years ago. Now we stood in almost silent anticipation outside the room where all our efforts, struggles and dreams of the past two years were to be realised, one way or the other.

We entered the room and almost silently settled ourselves into the now familiar single desks. "One more effort, that's all it will take, and then this will all be over." I was glad that the sane voice had accompanied me this morning.

The papers were handed out and we were instructed to turn them over. The first question concerned peripheral vascular surgery – one of my favourite surgical questions concerning care of the patient following varicose vein surgery. My heart began to beat less wildly and I felt a surge of relief as I pencilled out a brief summary of the main points so that I would not miss anything too important in the following essay.

Questions followed concerning care of specific wounds, intravenous infusions, recovery of a patient following general anaesthesia, stoma care, emotional care of patients following traumatic surgery such as amputation . . . and so the list went on. I was still writing when we were given the one-minute warning that the exam was due to finish.

"Time is up, ladies. Please stop writing and put your pens down."

A loud sigh resounded around the room. Relief etched with exhaustion lined every face. It was over. For better or for worse, the exams were over; we could now relax for a little while, because the results would not be known for at least a couple of weeks.

"Are you going to join us for a bevy, Hilary?" It was Belinda's voice. We had never really got on that well through the training and it was a lovely gesture for her to ask me to go to the pub with them. For some reason, though, an almighty bout of homesickness came over me and, almost crying, I made my apologies and rushed back to the nurses' home.

I didn't want to see or talk to anyone. I felt completely drained and numb. What had all this been about? All the hours of lifting patients and carrying bedpans, of testing samples of urine and faeces in the company of the bedpan washer in the sluice, of changing urinary catheter bags which smelled of old fish and, worse still, having them spill over your uniform and shoes. Of facing angry, grieving relatives, and laying out the dead, in the dark and alone, and trying to persuade paranoid patients that the medication you were attempting to give them was for their good and not an attempt on their life. Of being humiliated publicly at the whim of senior nurses who should have known better, and having to smile politely as yet another person vomited all over your clothes.

At that moment, I wondered why I had ever tried to become a nurse. I wept bitterly, out of sadness, because it had taken all that I had in me to get this far, and also out of relief that I had managed to survive.

When the tears finally dried, I sat at my desk and wrote a letter home. The evening shadows began to fall and, outside, large thundery drops of rain splashed liberally down. Taking the letter, I put on my jacket and went out into the rain. Having posted it, I then walked for miles, past Princes Street and out towards Arthur's Seat. The air was thick, wet and sticky, and my clothes were saturated, but I didn't care. I felt numb and saddened, disillusioned with my choice of career and frightened that I would never make it all the way.

Sitting down on a bench, the tears came again. And, sitting alone in the pouring rain, I asked the Lord to help me once again. After a while, the rain stopped and a gentle warm breeze ruffled the grass under my feet. I looked up and a shard of evening sunlight pierced the heavy clouds. For a moment, all that lay beneath it was transformed by its golden hue. All was soft and lovely. A skylark was singing somewhere high above and its song was joined by another. I couldn't see them, but I knew that they were there, dancing through the air, catching an evening snack before sleeping for the night.

The birds knew what to do, so surely I should. I stood up and began to walk back to the Infirmary. By the time I arrived, dusk was settling over the grey stone buildings. Lauriston Place was still a hive of activity as taxi after taxi brought anxious relatives to visit their loved ones. I looked up at the golden glow coming from the ward windows and caught sight of bobbing caps as nurses rushed up and down the wards.

The grandeur of the buildings, which had stood there for 250 years, felt hollow and unwelcoming and, as I looked at the Infirmary, it felt more like a foe than a friend. But I was too tired to care any more. Finding my way to my room, I fell into bed and slept until morning.

The following day, I was rostered to work on the first of my two pre-registration wards. We had been advised to choose one three-month placement for medical experience, and one for surgical. Surprisingly, and in what could only have been a moment of rash defiance, I had chosen to return to peripheral vascular surgery for my surgical placement.

This time, as I approached the ward, I was wearing three stripes on my hat and was hoping that this might just command a little more respect than previously. Climbing the stairs, I felt the familiar dread combined with determination. "I can do all things through Christ who strengthens me." The words which had carried me through so much already were becoming my mantra.

A few more "Help!" prayers, and I found my way through the two sets of double doors and on to the ward. Sister Dunblane was at her desk and didn't look up when I moved alongside the nurses' station.

"Good afternoon, Sister."

She continued to write her reports. "Is it?" She stood up and walked out of the ward.

I was left at the nurses' station, with a creeping regret moving up from my stomach to my throat.

Sally, one of the staff nurses, was more welcoming. "So you've decided to come here for your pre-reg then?"

"Yes, I loved the work when I was here as a junior student."

"Why are you looking so worried, then?" Sally was very perceptive.

"I just think that Sister does not like me at all and I don't know what I should do about it."

"Och, don't you worry about that. Sister is always a wee bit harsh with the students – it's just her way." She turned to answer a patient's buzzer and I surveyed the spotless ward with slightly less fear than before.

Report came and went, and I watched as a junior nurse was put through her paces by Sister's probing questions. I took notes and attempted to clear my brain of all the clutter of the past couple of weeks of exams.

I had been allocated the care of five patients who had had surgery for widely differing conditions. The most serious of my charges was a 60-year-old gentleman who had returned from theatre that morning following a below-knee amputation of one of his legs.

Mr Marsh was a lovely man and he was so appreciative of all the care that was given to him. For this sort of a patient, nothing was too much trouble.

It was good to be back at the bedside again and I began to feel more confident of my abilities to plan care and execute it in a thorough and knowledgeable way. It was lovely to hear the patients talking about the great care that they had received from all of the nurses; I felt proud to be included in that.

The shift continued with frequent post-operative observations of temperature, pulse rate, respiratory rate, and blood pressure, as well as observation of the wound site and ensuring that all the intravenous infusions were running at the correct rate. It sometimes felt a bit like a circus performance where somebody attempts to keep as many plates as possible revolving on vertical poles, ensuring that none of the plates fall to the ground.

Sister went home at about five o'clock and the atmosphere on the ward relaxed visibly. Sally busied about and made herself available if any help was needed. The junior student, Nicky, was having some difficulty with one of her infusions; together we managed to sort out the correct rate of flow.

At teatime, the evening meals came around in a huge stainless steel trolley which was pre-heated. We rushed up and down the ward with plates of food and, whilst we were doing this, one of the patients on the other side of the ward suddenly threw his plate on the floor and began convulsing.

With one mind, we all rushed to the bedside and hastily drew the curtains around Mr Davies's bed. His colour was awful; he was bright puce. We cleared the bed and locker area, and removed the head of the bed. He was recovering from surgery to his varicose veins, was due to be discharged the following day and had, as far as we knew, no other health worries.

Sally telephoned the crash team as Nicky and I attempted to keep poor Mr Davies on the bed, as he was in danger of throwing himself on to the floor. He was unable to breathe and the hypoxia was causing him to have a seizure. As the team arrived, I was instructed to attempt to reassure the other patients and their relatives, and to continue serving out the food.

I felt more than silly trying to pretend that all was normal, but there were hungry patients to attend to, so I carried on serving the meal. Elbows jutted out from behind the curtain, and voices kept speaking in hushed tones.

"I don't think that he has actually arrested."

"The problem seems to be in his throat."

"More suction, please."

There followed the familiar gurgling sound of the suction machine, and then a surprising "pop".

"There it is!" came the triumphant cry. "It's a Brussels sprout!"

Poor Mr Davies had inhaled a Brussels sprout: his trip to hospital had almost caused him to choke to death. Hospital food isn't all that bad, surely!

Mr Davies regained consciousness quickly and was rather surprised to find so many anxious faces around his bed. His throat also felt rather tender, unsurprisingly.

A very amused and relieved crash team came out triumphantly from behind the curtains and, as they cleared the debris and restocked their emergency trolley, there were some wry smiles and laughter.

The rest of the patients continued to look anxiously on, but as the curtains were pulled back and a happy, though slightly dishevelled, Mr Davies came into view, the anxiety turned to relief. There was an almost corporate sigh. All was well and, as Mr Davies explained to his neighbour in the next bed, he had never been very fond of the Brussels sprout in the first place.

Following the Brussels sprout arrest, the remainder of the shift went smoothly enough and Nicky regained her composure, keeping an extra-special eye on Mr Davies. When the night shift came on duty, we were each encouraged to give report on our patients. This always worried me because I didn't want to miss out any important information for the next shift.

Eventually, we went off duty. It felt satisfying to have returned to the wards and to have given hands-on care once again. Perhaps nursing was not so bad after all.

It was with a lighter heart that I returned to the ward at 7:30 the following morning. Sister, however, was on duty and, with her usual icy indifference, managed to extinguish the small glow of confidence that had begun to rekindle.

"Nurse McIntosh! What exactly do you call this bed?"

I looked at one of the corners on Mr Marsh's bed. It was slightly uneven, compared with the one on the other side. Mr Marsh, however, was washed, shaved and in clean pyjamas. His hair was combed and his intravenous infusion was running like clockwork. He was free from pain and was sitting happily in bed, feeling so much better than the night before. I was happy with the care I was giving him, and so was he. I really could not see where the problem lay.

Sister came over to the bed in a menacing fashion. "Don't they ever teach you students how to make beds any more?" Her voice was heavy with contempt.

"Yes, Sister, they do."

"Then why don't you bother to do it properly?"

"It is done properly, Sister, but one side is just a little longer than the other."

"Don't you answer back, you impudent girl! Now make the bed again!"

I looked at Mr Marsh. He could see the hurt on my face. "Don't worry, hen. I think she must have got out o' her bed the wrong side this morning."

His smile and compassion helped immensely, but I could feel the hot poker of indignation running its finger down my spine, all the way to a chilled stomach. Why could she just not leave me alone? Why was it so important to her to humiliate me at every turn?

I remade the bed, feeling as if the entire ward must be watching the event. It was embarrassing and, as I went to the linen cupboard to return the unused items, I felt hot tears at the back of my eyes. It all seemed so unjust. If I had done something wrong, then I could understand it, but I had been doing a good job. I knew what I was doing and I was doing it well.

Taking a deep breath, I returned to the ward and set about another sequence of observations. All the patients seemed to be doing well. But as I moved from patient to patient, my seething mind filled with revengeful thoughts. I fantasised about shouting at Sister from the middle of the ward and telling her a few home truths about her attitude.

Again the sane mind came to the rescue: "You mustn't give in to a bully. You must not stoop to her level. If you do, you will be the loser. The best thing is to pretend that it has not hurt you and to carry on and do your job to the best of your ability."

Eventually, the anger gave way to the sane mind and I calmed down. My patients were all behaving well and all of their observations were fine. The shift passed and, with less fear and more resolve, I went off duty, determined to return without fearing what this woman would say to me next.

Chapter Fourteen

"Now, what have I told you about your three-point turns, Hilary?" Eric's usually unruffled demeanour was showing signs of fraying around the edges. I looked blankly at him from the driver's seat.

"But I did turn the wheel one way and then the other, just as you said."

"I don't know what it is about you women, but you all do the same thing: you turn the wheel the same way twice."

Sitting in the the little Datsun Cherry with the summer sunshine beaming through the window, I tried to get to grips with the concept of three-point turns, but my mind just wasn't on the task. The results of the exams were due tomorrow and, no matter how hard I tried to pretend it wasn't happening, I just could not overcome the sense of dread and fear which kept creeping up on me.

"Come on, hen. I can see that we're not going to get much out of you today. Let's go home."

I turned the car and promptly stalled the engine. "Sorry, Eric. I'll be better next time, I promise."

Lighting another cigarette and opening the passenger window wide, he sighed ruefully. "Well, I do hope so. Your test is next week." As if I needed reminding.

Back at the nurses' home, Shahida and I had planned to meet up with Judith, one of the girls in Shahida's group. We spent a wonderful evening recounting tales of the bizarre things that had happened during the day's activities on the wards.

Judith had been working on one of the surgical wards when a patient who had been transferred from a neighbouring psychiatric hospital had become very disturbed. He had awoken from his appendicectomy, had promptly pulled out his intravenous infusion, and had attempted to bolt out of the ward, wearing only a theatre gown, which was wide open all the way up the back.

Judith, a staff nurse, and the house officer had all run in hot pursuit and had just managed to retrieve their patient before he made it to the final set of double doors, which opened on to the sedate, chequerboard corridors.

Retrieving him was one thing, but it was entirely another to coax him back to his bed. And all the while, he was bleeding quite freely from the IV site. Judith had compressed the bleeding site as best as she could, but it was a challenge to apply a bandage to the area, as his arms were spinning like windmills. The senior house officer was called and duly arrived with a large syringeful of largactyl. This was injected hastily in an attempt to calm the patient and to prevent any post-operative injury.

The medication took a while to take effect, but when it did, this gentleman was assisted back to his bed in a wheelchair and was left to sleep for the next few hours, with Judith on special alert in case of a repeat performance.

Shahida had been on duty on one of the medical wards and had had the opportunity to escort a patient to another hospital whilst he underwent a body scan. This had involved transporting the patient in an ambulance and it was at this point that Shahida had discovered that she did not travel well in this way.

When they arrived at the hospital, Shahida was feeling pretty wobbly. Just as she was reassuringly leading her patient out of the ambulance, she tipped sideways and banged her head on the side of the door.

Unruffled, and in a most professional manner, she proceeded to escort her patient to the relevant department, whilst sporting a very sizable "egg" on the side of her head. By the time the swelling had finished enlarging, her paper cap was listing slightly.

"I felt such a fool," she giggled. "There I was, all dressed up with my red cape blowing in the breeze, and then I toppled over and hit my head!" We were all laughing hysterically at this. After all, so many bizarre things had happened to us all.

We chatted on into the night, drinking cup after cup of coffee – all black because the fridge-raider was on the loose again and none of us had any milk left at all. It didn't matter; we were just glad to be able to share this time together, especially me, because my results were due out in the morning.

I was just about to get up to leave Shahida's room when she suddenly said, "Have you met the new nursing officer, Hilary?"

"No, should I have?"

"Well, she lives in the senior nurses' rooms just beyond your set of double doors. She's a Christian and her name is Laura Somerville. She's really lovely and only moved over here from Ireland a couple of weeks ago. She introduced herself to me as the leader of the Hospital Christian Fellowship and she has asked some of us round to her rooms for a tea party the day after tomorrow. Would you like to come?"

"If I'm still here by then," I grimaced.

"Oh, do shut up – you'll be fine. Judith and I have got our exams still to come, but you've finished yours. Just think, you are a free woman."

With that thought in my mind, I left Shahida and made my way back to my room. A free woman . . . or was I a condemned one? Only time would tell.

And that time was coming faster than I had wanted. Some people think that not knowing something is better than knowing it. At this point, I was falling into the former category. The thought of confronting that envelope in the morning was having a very detrimental effect upon my sleep.

By the time the morning came, I was entwined in a bed which would undoubtedly have won the Turner Prize. I hurriedly went for a bath and for the thousandth time wondered why on earth ten baths should have been placed in these awful, black-sided cubicles.

Dressing hurriedly, I began to make my way over to the post office in the main hospital building where we always collected our mail. Several of the other girls in my set were there already.

"Hullo, Jenny, how are you?"

Jenny giggled nervously. "I'll be a lot better when this is over. Did you get any sleep last night?"

"Not much," I admitted. "When are they going to open this place? Don't they know that it's Results Day?"

With that, the shutter was raised and we were allowed to enter. We all rushed towards the pigeonholes and sorted through the relevant ones.

"Here's yours, Jenny." I handed her envelope to her. Then, in my shaking hands, I saw my own name. "Oh, Lord, please let this be good news," I prayed silently.

Jenny began to jump and shout, "I've done it! I've done it! Oh, dear God, I don't believe it!" Then, hugging all and sundry, she dashed off to find a phone to let her family know the good news.

My white envelope stared at me challengingly from my trembling and sweaty-palmed hands. My stomach seemed to rise up into my chest, and my heart was thudding so loudly that I couldn't hear myself think.

Taking a deep breath, or six, I began to tear the envelope, carefully at first and then with increasing desperation. "Please let this be good news, please, please . . ."

And then, there in front of my eyes:

Dear Miss McIntosh,

I am pleased to inform you that you have been successful in your recent state final exams . . .

"Oh, dear God, I've done it, I've really done it! Thank you, Lord!"

All the other girls were tearing away at their envelopes and leaping for joy, and then running to find a phone. I stood in the corridor, watching. All that we had been through, all that we had seen and done, had not been in vain after all.

I ran back to my room and wrote a letter home, telling my parents the good news. Walking out into the summer sunshine to post it, my heart was suddenly full of relief and thankfulness. No more exams for the foreseeable future, and the opportunity of a good job at the Infirmary if that is what I chose to do.

It was as if my confidence had suddenly, and finally, been released. As I watched the staff nurses walking importantly through the hospital grounds, I thought, That's going to be me in a few months' time. The thought filled me with a mixture of delight and sheer terror.

It wasn't long before I was preparing to go on duty for the late shift which began at one o'clock. As I walked on to the ward, Sally smiled broadly. "I take it that it was good news, then?"

"Yes, and I can't believe it!"

"Well done! Do you think that you will be able to think straight today?"

"I'm not sure, but I'll do my best."

With that, I walked through the double doors and was greeted by Sister's stony stare.

"Nurse McIntosh has been successful in her state finals, Sister," said Sally.

"Right," she said, "let's get on with report. We've got a ward to run here, not a self-congratulatory party."

Not even Sister's indifference could ruin the elation I felt and, as we took report, my mind kept wandering to home. How I wished that I could share my good news face to face with my parents!

"Nurse McIntosh, you will special Mr McAulay in the side room. He has undergone surgery to repair a dissecting aortic aneurysm and has a "Y" graft in place. He will need special care, as we fear that the graft may be occluding, and his pedal pulses are extremely difficult to palpate."

Back on planet earth, I followed Sister into the little side room and was introduced to Mr McAulay and his wife, who sat by his bedside with reddened eyes and tell-tale streaks of mascara across her soft and kindly cheeks.

As Sister left the room, I set about making Mr McAulay as comfortable as possible. I checked that the IVs were running according to schedule and that hourly urinary output via a catheter was satisfactory.

"I'm just going to check for those pulses in your feet, Mr McAulay, if that is OK."

"You can do what the heck you like, Nurse. I couldn't care less any more."

"Now, now, Jimmy, don't be like that," said Mrs McAulay. "The nurse is only doing her job."

I felt the cold, grey feet for the pedal pulses, but it was extremely difficult to ensure that the pulses I was feeling were not those in my own fingers. I finally found a satisfactory pulse on both feet, but it was obvious that the feet were not very well perfused with blood, from their temperature and colour. I marked the area where it was possible to palpate a pulse with a cross, to make it easier to find next time.

"I have found a pulse in both feet, Mr McAulay, so that is good news. I will keep on checking them every half an hour or so, just to see if there is any change."

"Thank you, Nurse." Mrs McAulay smiled bravely. "That's good news, Jimmy. Everything will be all right, now." Jimmy looked far from convinced.

Throughout the afternoon, he dozed on and off whilst his wife, Janice, kept her bedside vigil. At three o'clock I asked the ward auxiliary to bring her a cup of tea, as she looked totally exhausted. The tea seemed to revive her a little and, as her husband slept, Janice explained to me how active her husband had been in his younger years.

"He used to play all sorts of racket games and was very good at them all. At the weekends he would play golf and go hiking; he was always out in the fresh air. The doctors have said, though, that it's the smoking which may have weakened his blood vessels and it is probably that which has made him so ill."

She gently ran her fingers across her husband's pale forehead. "He wouldn't stop smoking, you see, even when I told him that it could kill him. He wouldn't even cut down a little – he's a very determined man, you see."

I smiled at her and took her hand. "We'll do everything we can to help Jimmy get better, I promise you that."

The tears welled up again and I passed her a box of tissues. "Oh, what am I going to do? I couldn't bear to lose him – we've been through so much together." Janice wept quietly into her tissue and I gently rubbed her shaking shoulders.

The side room door opened: "Go for your break, Nurse McIntosh." It was Sister.

"I'll go in just a moment, Sister."

She glowered at me: "You will go when I tell you to."

Without wanting to create a scene, I crouched next to Janice's chair and, wiping a few wet strands of hair away from her forehead, I whispered, "I'll be back in a few minutes – I won't be long."

She squeezed my hand: "Thank you, Nurse."

With that, I explained all my observations to Sister and quietly left the room. I felt anger welling up inside my stomach, as I walked quickly down the corridor to the canteen to get a quick cup of coffee. I was angry because Sister had once again undermined me at a very important moment.

"What am I supposed to do with her, Lord?" The thoughts were jumbled in my mind.

"Just do your job. Just love the people I have given into your care, and I will sort out the rest." The answer came with a precious sense of peace which passes description. Feeling more hopeful, I returned to the ward and resumed my care of Jimmy and Janice.

At five o'clock, Jimmy was awake again and he was very uncomfortable. I alerted Sally and we drew up some analgesia, double-checking the dosage written on the drugs chart and countersigning the chart and the controlled drugs book. The injection, given intramuscularly, took a few minutes to take effect but, when it did, Jimmy was noticeably more relaxed.

I took the opportunity to give him a mini-bedbath and freshen-up. I cleaned his mouth, as he was still unable to eat or drink anything in case he should need to return to theatre. I changed the draw sheet underneath him and replaced the top sheet. I then combed his hair and, with this, his spirits improved markedly.

His wound sites were fine, but the pedal pulses were giving me cause for concern. The one on his right foot was now not palpable and, although all his other observations were satisfactory, I asked Sally to contact the senior house officer to alert him to the problem.

I explained the situation to Janice and Jimmy, and within a few minutes, Dr Montgomery had swept into the room to assess the situation for himself.

"Is this where you have been able to feel a pulse?"

"Yes, I've marked it with a cross. The pulse was palpable there half an hour ago, but it isn't now."

"I can feel that. How are his other obs?"

"They are all stable but his blood pressure dropped

slightly after the analgesia given at 5 p.m. It's now 110/70, pulse 76/minute."

"I'm not very happy with this situation, Mr McAulay," said the doctor, "and I'm going to get in touch with the senior registrar. I'm afraid that this may mean another trip to theatre, just to try to find out what is going on. Meanwhile, I'll ask one of the radiographers to bring a portable ultrasound machine up here, so that we can assess the blood flow through the graft."

"Thank you, Doctor." Janice's face was crumpling again, but she was trying bravely to keep smiling.

"Keep him nil by mouth," Dr Montgomery told me, "and let me know if there are any changes." With that, the doctor left the room.

I busily performed another set of observations and tried desperately to find the pulses in Jimmy's feet, which were now even colder and greyer than before.

Trying not to look worried, I bustled about, adjusting the flow rate on the IV and making sure that the fluid balance chart added up, and that Jimmy was not going into any form of retention of body fluids, which would make his condition even more precarious.

Fifteen minutes later, the radiographer arrived with her portable ultrasound machine. In those days, the machines were large and cumbersome; it was a struggle to get the machine into the small room and past all the other equipment which was already there. With a little adjustment, the machine was in place and the radiographer, along with Dr Montgomery, took a look at the "Y" graft.

The news was not good, as the graft appeared to have kinked and sagged. It was this which was causing the occlusion and limiting the blood supply to Jimmy's legs.

The senior registrar arrived and the little room seemed overwhelmingly full of white coats and machines. I kept my hand on Janice's shoulder as she sat and anxiously watched the screen and the faces of the medical team.

Dr Stewart broke the silence. "Mr McAulay, it looks as though the graft is not maintaining its proper shape, for some reason, and it is not allowing sufficient blood to flow down to your legs. I'm afraid that we are going to have to take you back to theatre now and we will try to put this right."

Jimmy sighed. "Do I have to do this today?"

"I'm afraid so, otherwise you could lose both of your legs, and even your life."

Janice's hand flew to her mouth. "Oh, no!" Again, she bit her lower lip and bravely kept control. "Well, Jimmy, there's nothing for it. You're going to have to go back in."

They exchanged glances and Jimmy nodded tiredly. "OK, just give me the form and I'll sign it." A consent form was hastily found and Jimmy signed on the dotted line.

Within ten minutes, I had prepared Jimmy for theatre and he was trundling down the cathedral-like corridor on his way to Theatre 10. I stayed with Jimmy whilst the general anaesthetic was administered; he held tightly on to my hand until he became unconscious. Janice was at his other side and, as Jimmy was intubated, I led her carefully away.

As we left the anaesthetic room, her sobs could be heard echoing in the arched ceilings. "What am I going to do? He will be all right, won't he?"

I tried to be as reassuring as possible, but I couldn't promise that all would be well. Once again, the stock phrase "The doctors are doing all that they can" came into play. As we walked back to the ward, my heart was in my stomach. I knew that the outlook was not good for Jimmy and I think that Janice knew this in her heart of hearts as well.

I advised Janice to go home and try and get some rest, or at least something to eat, as she was going to need all of her strength over the next few hours. I telephoned her son, who lived in Dalkeith, and asked if he could come to collect his mother and take care of her. Rory arrived about 20 minutes later and took Janice home. I was relieved to see that he had a kindly face; he immediately gave his mother an enormous hug and led her gently away.

Two hours later, we had the worst news from theatre. Jimmy had arrested on the operating table and the staff had been unable to revive him. With this news came that indescribable feeling which accompanies the knowledge that you have been with someone as they have gone on their journey into the next life. The shift came to an end and, as I left the ward, I met Janice and Rory at the entrance of the ward.

"I'm so very sorry, Janice," I said. Rory kept his arm protectively around his mother's shoulders. Tears were running freely down both of their faces.

"Th-thank you so much for all that you did to make Jimmy comfortable. No one could have done more."

A lump rose in my throat. "I'm so very sorry that I could not do any more." The tears were pricking at the back of my eyes. I touched them both on the arm and simply said, "Jimmy was a very lucky man to have such a lovely family."

With that, we parted and I trod wearily home, the memory of Jimmy, Janice and Rory deeply imprinted upon my heart.

Chapter Fifteen

The tea party in Laura Somerville's rooms was a sumptuous affair. The coffee table was laden with an assortment of cakes and biscuits, and we were offered coffee in bone china cups with saucers. The rooms themselves were large and spacious, but there was still an air of austerity in the proliferation of dark wooden panels, doors and floors, which Laura's pretty trinkets could only partially counterbalance.

We were welcomed with real warmth. I could see by Laura's demeanour that she was a woman used to maintaining the highest standards of order and cleanliness. She wore a pretty cameo brooch on the collar of her slightly frilly blouse. Her hair was slate grey and framed a face which seemed the picture of serenity. In the dark brown eyes I could see years of compassion combined with humour and I was immediately struck by the soft Irish accent when she welcomed us into her home.

Shahida, as always, was totally relaxed. Nothing seemed to faze her and she immediately sat down, crossed her legs and asked for a cup of coffee. I hovered around, waiting to be told to sit down. Authority figures were still a big hurdle for me and, in spite of everything, I still felt that I had to be on my best behaviour.

"Do sit down, please."

"Thank you. You have made this room look lovely. I love your ornaments," I gabbled on nervously. "Do you need any help with the drinks?" I said, whilst jumping out of the chair.

"No, no, it's all right. You just rest your weary bones; I

can manage the drinks – it was a double brandy you ordered, wasn't it?"

I glanced across the room to Shahida for support, only to find that she was trying to smother another of her rib-tickling laughs. I felt myself blush and simply said, "Oh, dear".

"I understand that you got your results yesterday, Hilary?" Laura carried on talking whilst she poured the coffee.

"Yes, I did."

"And I understand that congratulations are in order."

"Thank you. I still can't really believe that I've passed. I keep thinking that someone is going to tell me that they have made a mistake and that I'll have to resit the exams."

"You should have more confidence in yourself," Laura said. "If you believe, then anything is possible."

With that, Laura turned her attention to Judith, who was eyeing up the plate of scones. "Please help yourselves. You don't have to stand on ceremony here, you know."

We all began to work our way through the plates of goodies; Shahida and Laura talked about the Hospital Christian Fellowship and the planned forthcoming events. Sitting listening to them, I marvelled at Shahida's composure and confidence. I think that it was at that moment that I knew that she would be destined for great things. I wished that I could be more like her.

At this point, Maggie began to speak. Maggie was an enrolled nurse who worked in the Renal Unit at the Royal. She was effervescent and had the most infectious laugh. She had only recently become a Christian and was in the process of sorting out a lot of personal issues. Maggie had lots of questions about how faith can be put into action; she was a very practical person.

I listened avidly as Shahida and Laura carefully talked through many life issues, especially those regarding personal relationships.

"I've known my boyfriend for four years now and we've been living together, on and off, for three of those years.

Why is it that Christians say it is wrong to have sex before marriage?"

"Jesus says that before we enter into a physical relationship, we need to be totally committed to that person. Marriage is an expression of that commitment. We need to respect our body and that of our partner and make sure that our relationship is not just based on the physical, but that we are sure that we are there for them in every sense – emotionally, mentally and physically." Laura was speaking in her quiet way and a hush had come over the room.

Maggie's face flushed. "Do you think that I might have to change things, then?"

"I think that it would be a good idea to talk to your boyfriend and explain that you have come to understand that your life belongs to Jesus now and that you want to do what honours him the most. After all, Jesus always leads us in the way that is ultimately best for us, although it is not always the most simple of ways."

Shahida added, "And you can be sure of that, Maggie, because he loves you so much that he went to the cross to die in your place."

"I know that." Maggie's voice was almost a whisper: "I can never understand why he did that."

"He did it for every single person on this planet. I don't think that any one of us could possibly begin to understand the incredible love that God has for people. All he wants us to do is to begin to love and trust him too, and to follow where he leads us." Laura's face was bright as she talked and I think that we all sensed that the issues being discussed were important to us all.

The evening came to an end and we all went our separate ways. I felt comforted to know that Laura was only a few doors away – it was good to have met her at last and to have laid some of the "authority figure" fears to rest.

The following day was a day off duty and I woke at about eight o'clock to hear the rain falling heavily against the window. I turned over in bed and attempted to fall asleep again. For some reason, I just could not drift off. I kept telling myself that there was nothing planned for that day and that I could relax and take it easy, but still there was a nagging thought at the back of my mind that I should get up.

Another ten minutes passed and by this time, I was wide awake. "OK, Lord, you win." I crawled out of bed and headed for the bathroom. A soothing soak in the bath should surely do the trick. Whilst in the bath, though, I kept thinking that I really should go out, but where? I had not planned to visit anyone that day and had decided that this day would be given to doing some mundane washing and shopping.

Still the uneasiness persisted. "Well, if you want me to go out, where do you want me to go?" By this stage, I was towelling myself dry and halfway through cleaning my teeth. A single word popped into my mind: "Morningside."

Morningside is a very nice suburb of Edinburgh; I would sometimes walk out that way to visit some of the shops. I had no idea why I should go that way on this day, but I decided that, if that was where I was supposed to go, then who was I to argue?

Dressing hastily and with a sense of mounting anticipation, I set out on my walk. The rain was easing by now, but the wind was still strong and lazy. I clasped my raincoat around me as I walked up the hill into the head wind. I do feel a fool, I thought. What on earth am I doing here?

Halfway up the hill there was a bus stop and, standing in its shelter, I could see the figure of a young woman. For some reason, I thought that I recognized her as one of my colleagues from the Infirmary. She turned to look in my direction and I could see that she was smiling, so I waved to her and she waved in return.

"Speak to her." The voice was most insistent.

"But what on earth should I say?" I asked silently. By now, I was almost within speaking range of the young woman.

"Tell her about me,"came the voice again. My heart leapt in a mixture of fear and embarrassment. The face in front of me was still smiling, but I could see that the smile only thinly disguised sadness and pain.

"Hullo," I said. "Do I know you? I feel sure that I've met you somewhere."

"'Ello." The accent was undeniably French. "Zat is really strange, because I thought that you were someone I knew, too."

"Are you going into town?" I asked, not knowing what to say to either a positive or negative answer.

"Yes, I am. I am going to buy a birthday present for the little boy I am an au pair for."

"Oh, that's lovely," I said. We stood there in the howling wind and I felt that if I did not mention the Lord somehow, then I would burst. "My church is in town," I said. "It's just behind Princes Street."

"Oh," she said, "zat's nice."

"I'm so grateful for my church." I was getting into my stride now. "My parents are in Hong Hong, you see, and I really needed somewhere where I would feel accepted and loved. I am so glad that Jesus is real and that he cares for every one of us."

There. I had said it. I could feel my palms sweating in spite of the cutting wind, and I was finding it difficult to understand why I had to speak to this poor girl in a howling gale, standing in an inhospitable bus shelter. Fully expecting her to tell me to leave her alone, I prepared to walk away.

"Thank you," she said. "Zat is one of the most wonderful things that I have ever heard."

Looking into her eyes, I could see that she was near to tears. Now it was her turn to unburden her heart.

"My name is Sophie. I came here from Lausanne eight weeks ago and I am so lonely. I miss home so much, but I cannot afford to return zere yet. Did you really mean it when you said zat Jesus loves all people?"

"Yes, I did. He really does and it doesn't matter what we have done in the past. All he asks of us is that we recognise our need of his forgiveness and come to him, asking him to come into our lives, so that we can begin a new life with him."

"Zat sounds too good to be true." Sophie looked doubtful. I could see her bus rising over the crest of the hill. I grabbed a pencil and paper from my handbag and hastily wrote down my name, address, and the telephone number of the hall phone; Sophie gave me her details in return.

"Please call me if you would like to speak again," I said as she climbed aboard the bus.

"I will," she said, "and zank you."

With that, Sophie left for town and I was left standing at the bus stop. The feeling of urgency had completely disappeared. "I guess it's back to the washing, then, Lord?" With that, I turned and walked towards home.

I didn't expect to hear from Sophie again and all the way home I became more and more convinced that what I had done had been wrong. By the time I arrived back at my room, I felt quite humiliated and ashamed. After all, what right did I have to try to force my own beliefs upon anyone else? Feeling miserable, I headed for the laundry with arms full of dirty washing and set about the task with dejected animation. The washing machines were broken again, so it was down to washing everything by hand and using the spin-dryer.

It took some time before the laundry was finished and I was more than ready for a cup of coffee by the time I returned to my room. As I opened the door, a little white slip of paper landed on the carpet. It was a note from reception which read, "Sophie came to see you at 10 a.m. and would like to speak to you. Please phone her at home."

Rummaging through the world's untidiest handbag, I eventually found Sophie's number and headed off down the corridor to call her.

"'Ello!" Sophie's unmistakable voice answered the phone.

"Hello Sophie, it's Hilary here. I'm sorry that I wasn't around when you came to visit."

"Zat is OK," she said. "It's just zat you said that if I needed to talk, zen I could call you?"

"Yes, of course! I'd love to help if I can."

"Do you sink zat you could come to visit me at zis house zis afternoon? I have to look after Thomas until two o'clock and zen I am free and I would love to talk more about Jesus. Is zat OK?"

Sophie gave me instructions on how to find her employer's home and I walked back to Morningside in time for two o'clock. All the way there, I was wondering what on earth I should do or say. I felt so ill-equipped. Arriving at the house, I simply prayed that the Lord would guide us both and help us.

Sophie answered the door and ushered me inside. She led me to an attic room which had an outstanding view across the city.

"This is beautiful, Sophie, and you have made your room look lovely."

"Merci," she said. "Would you like some coffee?"

I was wondering how on earth to get to the meat and bones of the conversation when Sophie took the plunge: "If Jesus can 'elp people, zen I really want 'im to 'elp me."

I sat looking at her, realising that the Lord had been preparing Sophie for a leap of faith. She talked about the previous few years in which she had been trying to find a purpose in life, but everything that she had tried had ended in disappointment. This included relationships, jobs, hobbies . . . everything had left her with a feeling of incompleteness and dissatisfaction.

Taking a deep breath, I explained that becoming a Christian means that we are willing to let Jesus be central to our life. That would mean replacing the "I want to do it my way" mentality with "What do you want me to do, Lord?"

I explained that although this was frightening at first, we had to trust Jesus. After all, he was the one who had been willing to go to the cross and die for us, to take away the penalty of our sin, so that we could be free. Surrendering to Christ was actually the way of freedom because we could never achieve it by our own futile efforts.

Sophie sat and listened quietly. When I had finished speaking, she simply said, "What do I have to do to come to know Jesus?"

"All you have to do is to say sorry for anything that may have been wrong in your life and to ask Jesus to come into your heart and become your Lord and Saviour."

"Do I have to say it out loud?" Sophie looked embarrassed.

"No. God knows exactly what is in your heart. You can speak to him in your heart if that is easier."

"OK."

With that, Sophie closed her eyes and remained quiet for a minute or two. I sat with her, praying that she would know that her leap of faith would be into the loving arms of God the Father.

Time passed. A single tear began to trickle down Sophie's cheek. She opened her eyes at last and smiled.

"I sink zat I have met with 'im. I felt all warm and 'appy in 'ere." Sophie was pointing to her heart. "For ze first time in ages I feel at, 'ow do you say?"

"At peace?" I suggested.

"Oui. At peace."

We talked on for a while and I explained to Sophie that it would be really helpful for her to find a supportive church where she would be helped and encouraged. She said that she would like to come to Charlotte Chapel and I arranged to meet her there on the following Sunday evening.

As I left the house, I felt amazed. It had been one of those special, God-ordained meetings where everything had been under his direction and for the benefit of all concerned. I was beginning to understand the truth that "in all things God works for the good of those who love him" (Romans 8:28). The day's events had left me totally in awe of him.

The following Sunday evening, Sophie found her way to the Chapel and really enjoyed the worship and the sermon, which just happened to be about Jesus searching for the lost sheep.

"I am zat sheep," Sophie whispered to me, "and I am so 'appy zat I 'ave been found."

The following week came the dreaded driving test. The morning dawned brightly but with the threat of later rain. As I opened the curtains in my room, the knot in my stomach was approaching the size of a basketball.

"Why do I keep putting myself through all these ordeals, Lord?" I was muttering anxiously to myself. The test was due to take place at two o'clock and I had a whole morning to try and fill with purposeful activity before then.

As I ate my porridge, most of which was still cemented on to the saucepan left soaking in the kitchen, I tried to revise the Highway Code. My brain cells were definitely on strike, as though they were in sullen refusal to absorb any more information. Braking distances were my worst thing. I just could not remember which distance related to which speed. All that I could remember was that the distances doubled in the rain. A rising sense of panic sent me in the direction of the laundry room. Whenever I needed to think, it helped to be either washing or ironing.

An hour later, all the laundry was finished and I was pacing up and down in my room. I decided to write a letter home. That always helped. Half an hour later, that was finished and I set out to post it at the hospital post office. It felt strange to be fearing something other than the hospital itself.

Eventually, one o'clock came and Eric arrived for my pre-test lesson. He was smiling broadly and the inevitable cigarette was burning in his hand.

"Hello, hen!" He leaped out of the car for me to get into the driver's seat. "How's it going today?"

I looked at him and smiled weakly, "Er, do I really have to do this thing, Eric?"

"Och, you'll be fine. I've put my money on you passin' t'day."

"Oh, no," I groaned quietly. As my hands touched the wheel, they slipped because of the moisture on my palms.

"C'mon, hen, let's hit the road. We've got to get your emergency stop sorted before two o'clock, so let's get a move on."

I set off from the hospital and turned left down the now familiar route which Eric had shown me over the past few weeks. We went out into the hilly suburbs and practised the reversing-around-a-corner-on-a-hill manoeuvre, which was very good for burning out the clutch. The hill start went OK and then we drove out further and found a quiet road on which to practise the emergency stop.

"Now, Hilary, when I hit the dashboard, I want you to bring the car to a stop, without stalling the engine. Remember to put the car in neutral and apply the hand-brake when the car has stopped."

That went quite well and before long, Eric was directing me to the test centre. It had started to rain. I had never had a lesson in the rain. For some reason, the weather had always been good for my lessons. I had to ask Eric where the windscreen wipers were and this really made me nervous. He wasn't looking so impressed either.

At the test centre, I waited in a small room with Eric until a short, dark-haired man came out of the office and called my name.

"I want to go home, I want to go home . . ." The words kept repeating through my mind.

"Now, Miss McIntosh, show me to your car, please." He had that no-nonsense, I'm-in-control sort of voice that parents use with their children when the children are getting on their nerves.

"It's, it's the white one, halfway up the road."

"The Datsun Cherry?"

"Er, yes, yes, that's right." I hoped that it was.

"Right. I'd like you to read the number plate of the blue car which is just behind yours."

I read the number plate.

"Right. Let's get on with the test."

I trotted up the road beside him and, remembering that Eric had said that he wanted to teach me to be a lady when driving, I opened the examiner's door before my own.

I sat down and fidgeted with the mirrors, seat belt, gear stick . . . anything that would possibly delay my having to drive in front of this officious man whom I did not know.

"Pull away when you're ready."

I looked in the wing mirror and the rear-view mirror, and over my shoulder, and waited until the road was clear before pulling out. I tried to listen to the engine to make sure that the revs were OK. The examiner took me out on all the routes which had become familiar with Eric. As we headed for the derestricted road, I accelerated up to 45 miles an hour. Eric had said that this was fast enough for a learner and I didn't dare go any faster.

It had stopped raining and I suddenly thought that it might be a good idea to turn off the windscreen wipers. I was just reaching for the lever when the examiner said that the windscreen had had enough of being wiped when it was bone dry.

We turned back into the suburban roads and headed for my famous reversing-around-a-corner-on-a-hill. I set the car in the right place for the manoeuvre and then used the accelerator and clutch to ease the car backwards, constantly checking all my mirrors.

Halfway through the manoeuvre, I realised that I was going to hit the kerb so I applied the brakes. Because we were on such a steep hill, the examiner's head and shoulders flopped forward as I stopped the car.

"I'm really sorry," I stammered, heaving up the handbrake. He said nothing but sat in stony silence as I attempted the procedure once again. This is it, I thought. I've failed now, for sure.

I felt a wave of sheer misery waft over me but tried to put it out of my mind as I coaxed the car around the corner, this time without decapitating the examiner. Next came the hill start, and this time, all went according to plan. The emergency stop went well and then we were on our way back to the test centre.

Parked outside, he showed me various road signs which I had to identify. The last one concerned turning right into a line of traffic turning the other way. By this stage, I just could not remember the rules concerning overtaking in the left-hand lane but it didn't seem to matter.

"Switch off the engine, please." I turned the key and felt my heart missing several beats. "Well, I'm pleased to tell you that you have passed."

"REALLY? Oh, thank you so much! I'm really sorry that I nearly bounced you through the windscreen on that reversing. Thank you so much! I can't believe it!"

Eric came out of the office, beaming. "I knew you could do it, hen. Now all you need to do is your advanced driving test."

"I think I need some time to recover from this one first, Eric, and thank you for all you've taught me."

Eric drove me back and, clutching my certificate, I ran up to my room to write my second letter home.

Chapter Sixteen

Back at the Infirmary, my pre-registration period was entering its final stage with a transfer to Male Medical on Ward 26. After all the stresses of life with Sister Dunblane on the ward, which had never really been resolved satisfactorily, it was a relief to change wards knowing that the end of my training was in sight.

It was autumn now and the colder winds and unexpected snow flurries had brought an overcapacity to the medical wards ahead of the regular winter crisis. As I entered the ward for the first time, I was struck by the pungent odour of urinary catheter bags, only thinly disguised by the smell of disinfectant.

The ward was very full and busy. Extra beds were added to the bays and the air was filled with the sound of men coughing productively. As I walked towards the nurses' station, an old man in a tartan dressing-gown sat wheezily next to an oxygen cylinder, whilst a nebuliser administered salbutamol in a fine mist via a face mask. It was impossible to distinguish any facial features as they were enshrouded in the vapour mist.

He looked up as I walked past. "Nurse!" I moved across to where he was sitting. "I need a pee. Get me a bottle, hen!"

I went to the nurses' station and quickly locked my handbag away before rushing down the full length of the ward to the sluice to collect a urinal bottle. When I returned, it was too late; Mr Burney was sitting in a puddle and his pyjamas and dressing-gown were soaked.

"Nurse McIntosh!" It was Sister's voice now. "Time for report."

I walked briskly up to Sister to explain Mr Burney's delicate situation and she quickly dispatched one of the nursing auxiliaries to help Mr Burney wash and change. I could tell that it was going to be a busy shift.

Sister ran through the patients' conditions with speed. It soon became obvious that we had thirteen patients who needed total care – they were unable to move themselves in bed at all, could not even use a commode to go to the toilet, and had to be fed. There were only three of us on duty and some of the patients were not expected to make it through the night.

At the end of the report, Sister concluded that, in spite of the ward being full to overflowing, it was supposed to be our evening "on take" and that we could expect to have up to three extra admissions during the course of the evening.

Staff Nurse Kerrigan was in charge and she delegated the bottom two bays of patients to my care. This included many of the patients who were doubly incontinent and who needed two-hourly pressure area care to prevent breakdown of the skin on the areas most under pressure when lying immobile in bed. The other member of staff was a first-year student nurse who was working with Staff Nurse Kerrigan. It was going to be hectic, to say the least.

As soon as the early shift left the ward, the buzzers started ringing as patients called for help. It was visiting time and a well-dressed woman had entered the ward with an enormous bouquet for her father. As I rushed to answer the buzzer, she held out the flowers in front of her and instructed, "Put those in water will you?" and, taking off her fine gloves, she settled down beside her father and began to talk to him.

Incredulous, I rushed off to the sluice to find a suitable vase. I regret to say that the flowers did not receive the treatment they deserved. The buzzers were going incessantly, so

I filled the vase with water and stuffed the foliage into it as quickly as possible before returning the offering to the gentleman in question. His daughter looked up disdainfully.

"There you go," I said. "What lovely flowers."

With that, I turned to assist Jack Meredith who had been sitting on the commode with the screens around him for the past 20 minutes.

Trying to freshen the air without causing someone embarrassment is a difficult task at the best of times, but it was verging on impossible at this moment in time. Jack had been on the ward for a long time and suffered with severe arthritis for which he was prescribed powerful painkillers containing a lot of codeine. This has the side effect of causing constipation. Jack had said that he had been having trouble with his bowels for four days now; it was unfortunate that his laxatives should begin to take effect right in the middle of visiting, when the ward was so full.

As I opened the curtains, it was not necessary to ask whether they had been effective. I took a deep breath and held it until I had successfully transferred Jack from the commode back on to his bed and had covered the commode once again.

"Just a moment, Jack. I'll just bring something back from the sluice."

I backed out of the curtained area and went in search of the can of air freshener. I did not want to open the curtains on the unsuspecting patient in the next bed without having freshened the air first.

Finding the can, I rushed back to Jack and casually sprayed around the commode and the air in general.

"This should do the trick," I said and with that, Jack began to cry. I sat on the bed next to him and held his hand. "Oh Jack, I'm so sorry. I didn't mean to upset you."

Jack found a handkerchief and blew his nose noisily. "It's all right, hen, I know that you're just doing your job.

It's just that I'm a useless waste of space in here. I want to go home."

"I know you do, Jack. The problem is that you're not well enough to go home just yet and we are here to help you. I'm sorry that the ward is so busy; it must be difficult to get any peace or privacy at the moment."

"Aye, that it is, hen. That it is."

"Have you any visitors coming in to see you this afternoon?"

"No. Nobody's coming until Helen, my wife, this evening."

"Would you like me to take you down to the television lounge for a little while? It might just give you a bit of a break from all these people and a bit of privacy."

Jack's face brightened. "Could you do that, hen? I know that you are really busy."

"It's no problem. Let me just get rid of the commode and then I'll bring a wheelchair and take you down."

Safely ensconced in the TV room, watching football, Jack turned to give me the thumbs up. He was smiling now and, for a little while at least, the embarrassment caused by the commode was forgotten. The buzzer went again. This time it was a relative of one of the CVA patients. CVA stands for "cerebral vascular accident" and is the technical name for a stroke.

Mr Barrie was critically ill – he was 84 years old and totally incapacitated by his condition. He could not eat, drink or move for himself and was barely conscious. Fluids were administered to him via an IV drip, but this was to prevent him dying from dehydration. He was not expected to live through the night; on his Kardex notes, written in large red letters, was NFR, or "not for resuscitation". This had all been discussed with his daughter, who was now sitting at his bedside.

"My father seems to be agitated," she said. "What is happening to him?"

I approached Mr Barrie and took hold of his free hand which was flailing about. "Mr Barrie? Mr Barrie, can you hear me?"

He opened half an eye. The hand moved down to his groin area and he moaned very weakly. I pulled back the bedclothes gently and, sure enough, the draw sheet underneath him was soaked with a mixture of urine and blood. There, lying in the bed, was the inflated balloon of the urinary catheter, which should have kept it in place. Mr Barrie must have pulled at the catheter with some force to have removed it.

"Oh, Mr Barrie, what have you done that for? That must have been very painful."

His daughter asked what the matter was and I tried to explain the situation as delicately as possible.

"Mr Barrie, I'll get you washed and change the sheet underneath you and then I'll contact the doctor and ask him to pop another catheter in for you."

I explained to Mr Barrie's daughter that a catheter was necessary to prevent constant soiling and subsequent breakdown of her father's skin in that area. She nodded sadly.

I washed her father gently and, moving him very carefully, changed the draw sheet underneath him. I cleaned and freshened his mouth which was very dry as he was unable to take fluids orally. I tried to make him as comfortable as possible before the doctor arrived. A few minutes later, another catheter was inserted and Mr Barrie seemed to fall asleep, with his daughter at his side.

The buzzers were still going. Sally, the other student nurse, asked me to come and help with one of her patients who was complaining of pain in one of his ankles. Mr Coulthard was complaining bitterly that he was so fed up that he wanted to die. We did our best to chivvy him along and I dashed to the TV room to find a footstool to make him more comfortable. From report, we had been told that he had cardiac problems and that he had been resident on the ward for several weeks, following the death of his wife. There was now nobody who could look after him at home and his symptoms were too severe for care in a nursing home, so the only place he could safely live now was on our ward.

I hurried back to Mr Coulthard's bed, carrying the footstool.

"There we are," I said. "That should make your ankles a little more comfortable."

Mr Coulthard grunted in return and turned his face away towards the window. Another buzzer was being pressed urgently, this time for Willie, another long-term resident of the ward. He had heard that there was an important football match on the TV and had decided that he would like to watch it. I walked briskly up to the top of the ward where a couple of wheelchairs belonging to the ward were parked. Just as I was about to wheel this down to Willie, Sally came running up to me: "Hilary! It's Mr Coulthard – I think he's arrested!"

"He can't have," I said stupidly. "I've only just given him a footstool."

Together we rushed down the ward, which was just emptying at the end of the afternoon visiting hour. Sure enough, Mr Coulthard sat slumped in his chair. He was colourless and pulseless and there was a large quantity of yellow vomitus down his chest.

"Oh, no!" I whispered. "Quick, Sally, shut the curtains on that side!"

As Sally pulled the curtains around the bed, I removed the head of the bed and moved the bed a little further from the wall. I pressed the emergency buzzer three times, the coded call system we used for such an emergency.

"You take his feet and I'll take his top," I instructed Sally and together we lifted Mr Coulthard on to his bed. It would have been easier to place him on the floor to attempt resuscitation, but there was not enough room to do so.

Grunting with the effort, we managed to lift our patient on to the bed.

"Get the arrest board, quickly!"

Sally ran off down the ward to find the board which was placed under the mattress to provide a firm surface so that external cardiac massage would be more effective. Meanwhile, Staff Nurse Kerrigan had come running and had called the crash team. I wiped the vomit away from Mr Coulthard's mouth and started attempting to clear his airway.

The next moment, the crash team arrived and Staff Nurse Kerrigan took over.

"Get on with the obs", she told me. "It looks like you'll have to do the lot yourself. Sally has just gone for her break."

With that, she shut the curtains and assisted the doctors in trying to bring Mr Coulthard back to life. As I walked off in search of my sphygmomanometer, or blood pressure machine, my own heart was thumping. I felt shocked that Mr Coulthard should have been relatively OK one minute and virtually dead the next.

A hush came over the ward. All of the patients were aware of what had happened and they seemed saddened and upset by it all. As I moved from one patient to the next, I attempted to make light conversation and to reassure them all. My hands were shaking as I applied the cuff to check each blood pressure.

"Ee, your hands are cold, Nurse." It was Eddie Burney, the man with the oxygen cylinder. "You look as if you've seen a ghost."

With that, he started to laugh and this, unfortunately started off another wheezing fit which took several minutes to subside.

"Just breathe gently Eddie." I tried to sound as if I was not panicking. "In and out, in and out, that's it. You're doing fine."

Eddie gave me a sideways glance as he fought to control his breathing. He was right; who was I trying to kid? I was taking much longer than usual over the obs (Sally was still on her break). The activity behind Mr Coulthard's curtains continued and I moved from patient to patient, checking temperature, pulse and respiration rate and blood pressure as quickly and efficiently as possible. But the buzzers kept sounding and a moment later there was the dreaded three-buzzes-in-a-row. According to the buzzer board at the nurses' station, it had come from the bathroom area.

I walked down the ward like a speed-walker, but I think that I would have been disqualified for jogging. Rushing into the toilet area, there was Alec McTighe.

"Och, hen," he said, "I cannae find the light switch. I thought that this was it, this red cord."

I didn't know whether to laugh or cry. 'It's OK, Alec," I said, "*this* is the proper light switch. The red one is for emergencies."

"Och, well," he said, "no wonder it didna work." With that, he shuffled into the cubicle and shut the door.

Going back into the main ward, I saw that the crash team were emerging from Mr Coulthard's curtains. I could tell by their rounded shoulders and quiet voices that all their efforts had been in vain. Staff Nurse Kerrigan looked at me and shook her head sadly.

"How far have you got with the obs?"

I explained Eddie's and Alec's antics and told her that I had not made as much progress as I would have hoped.

"That's OK," she said. "You go for your break and then you can lay out Mr Coulthard when you come back."

It was a relief to leave the ward for a few minutes, but the coffee lounge was a good five minutes' walk from the ward, and the afternoon coffee break was only meant to last fifteen, so it meant that no sooner had you sat down to drink, than you were up and hurrying back to the ward. As I sat down, I saw Shahida arriving for her break.

"How's it going?" she asked.

"Can't you see the steam rising from my feet?"

"Oh, it's a bit like that, is it?"

I gulped down the coffee. "I've got to dash, Shahida. I've got a date."

Shahida laughed. "You mean a dead cert?"

"How did you guess?!" Shahida knew that I hated laying out dead people, so we had devised this thinly veiled description to help us cope with one of life's eventualities.

As I returned to the ward, the Womens' Royal Voluntary Service trolley was doing the rounds and the ladies were selling sweets and newspapers. It was one of the highlights of the men's day and those who were able chatted to the ladies. Betty, the auxiliary, was serving teas from her trolley, but there were no nurses to be seen. The curtains around Mr Coulthard's bed remained closed, so I went in search of my colleagues down at the bottom of the ward.

The curtains around Mr Barrie's bed were now drawn and, as I peeped behind, I found Staff Nurse Kerrigan and Sally comforting his daughter. Mr Barrie was in the process of dying. His respirations were coming in rapid gulps which then seemed to fade away to almost nothing, only to begin again, building to a crescendo and then fading again. This was classic Cheynes-Stokes respirations which occurred when the patient's brain was failing to regulate respiratory effort.

Staff Nurse Kerrigan turned to me. "Will you see to Mr Coulthard now, Nurse McIntosh?"

I could see that the stress of the day was beginning to tell. There were still so many aspects of care needing to be completed, but we were making very little headway.

I nodded and went in search of the bathing trolley, filling the basin with warm water and, finding the only remaining mortuary gown and napkin, set off for Mr Coulthard's bed.

Behind the curtains, Mr Coulthard's body was cooling down quickly. Rigor mortis was setting in and I had some difficulty removing his pyjama top. I washed him gently and, as I always did, talked to him whilst I worked.

"Now Mr Coulthard, I'm just going to wash under your arms, that's it . . . and I'm just going to wash your back now, so I'll roll you over this way . . ."

As I rolled him, the remaining air in his lungs expired and he seemed to give a low moan. I was so frightened that I almost dropped him over the edge of the bed. Standing with my heart thudding and my knees shaking, I looked down at the pale figure under my hands. No, it was all right; he was dead. For another moment I stood and watched his chest. There was no movement there. I placed my hand on his chest to palpate a heart beat, but there was nothing.

Rolling his body back the other way, I washed the other side of his back and buttocks. Now came the tricky bit: I had to fold a nappy under his buttocks and then tie it at the front. It was a relatively easy procedure when done by two people, but it was very difficult when attempted alone, especially with the onset of rigor mortis.

By the time I had completed the procedure, applied the correct details to the toe label, and completed wrapping the body in a gown and shroud, another half-hour had passed. I felt exhausted from the sheer physical effort. I had tried so hard to make sure that Mr Coulthard had been treated with dignity and respect. As I tucked the shroud around his face, I said to him, "It's all right now, Mr Coulthard. You can be with your wife now."

Leaving the bed, I telephoned the mortuary technicians and advised them that there was a body to collect. Ten minutes later, the stainless steel trolley could be heard trundling down the main corridor. This was our cue to draw all the curtains around the other patients' beds, so that they would not have to see the body being removed.

"Where's yer man?" It was Charlie, who had worked in the mortuary for about 20 years but still seemed to have an irrepressible humour.

"He's over here," I said.

"OK, hen, leave him to us."

Charlie and his associate, who evidently did not share the same good humour, manoeuvred the trolley past the adjacent beds and lifted Mr Coulthard's body skilfully inside the stainless steel casket. I gathered all of Mr Coulthard's belongings into a plastic bag, compiling a brief inventory, for his family to collect. The trolley rumbled stoically out of the ward, and with that, we pulled back the curtains of the remaining patients. I stripped Mr Coulthard's bed, washed it clean, and then remade it.

The telephone rang. It was one of the house officers from Casualty.

"It's just to let you know that we have a patient for you . . . a middle-aged man with chest pains. CCU is full, so he's coming to you, OK?"

Whether it was OK or not, it seemed that Mr Coulthard's bed was not going to remain empty for very long.

I went in search of Staff Nurse Kerrigan to tell her the news and found that Mr Barrie had just passed away.

"I'll see to the admission, because he is likely to need close monitoring," she said. "You lay out Mr Barrie once the doctor has certified death and, in the meantime, help Sally finish the obs. God knows when we're going to get the medicine round finished."

"Would you like me to do that, once I've done the obs with Sally?"

"Do you think that you could manage that?"

"Well, I did the drugs round alone on night duty, so I'm sure it will be all right. I'll ask you if I'm not sure about anything."

Sally and I whizzed through the remaining observations and I pulled out the drugs trolley just as the new patient arrived, simultaneously with the dinner wagon. It was chaos. Sally helped to serve the meals, Staff Nurse Kerrigan admitted the gentleman with chest pain, and I manoeuvred past them all with the drugs trolley. Miraculously, all the patients were observed, fed and had their drugs correctly administered in record-breaking time.

Whilst the patients ate their meal, I hurried to the next ward to borrow a mortuary pack and then set up the bathing trolley once again to perform last offices for Mr Barrie. Once behind the curtains, I gently removed the IV line from his hand, and then his urinary catheter. I then set about giving him his final wash and dressed him in the mortuary gown, nappy and shroud. Mr Barrie's face was peaceful at last. I combed his hair and tried to imagine all the experiences of life he might have enjoyed – all the things that he had seen and heard, places he had visited.

My brief reverie was interrupted by Staff Nurse Kerrigan on the other side of the partition, where she was caring for our new admission.

"Oh drat! He's arrested!" came her stage whisper, followed by the sickening thud as the headboard was removed and landed on the floor.

"I'll get the team!" I called as I passed the bed, and shot off up the ward to the phone. My hands were shaking as I dialled the emergency number. The operator seemed to take an age to answer; maybe they were on their break.

"Come on, come ON!"

"Emergency team. Which ward?"

"Ward 26. We have a cardiac arrest."

"I'll send the team straightaway."

I threw down the receiver and hurtled off down the ward with the arrest board under one arm and pushing the crash trolley, which had only just been restocked, with the other hand.

Behind the curtains, Staff Nurse Kerrigan's usually immaculate auburn hair was flopping about her face as she knelt on the bed trying to compress her patient's heart. He was lying there looking very dead and the interminable, soulful, monotonous bleep of the cardiac monitor suggested that we were not progressing very well.

We slid the board under Mr Dalkenny's back and I rushed to get the oxygen cylinder from the top of the ward. As I did so, the outer doors of the ward swung open and three doctors, white coats splayed by the speed of their wearers, came briskly down the ward.

"What is it with you on this ward today?" said the house officer. "I thought we were supposed to help people live, not bump them off!"

With that, he disappeared behind the curtains. I placed the oxygen cylinder at the head of the bed, ensured that it was working, then left them all to do their work.

As I emerged from the curtains, Mr MacWhinney in the opposite bed gave me a reassuring smile. "It's been quite a day, hasn't it, Nurse?"

I tried to look calm and professional, but I found his sympathy had caught me by surprise. I bit my lower lip which, I have to admit, was beginning to tremble. "I think that we can safely say that it has, Mr MacWhinney."

I called the mortuary again and advised them that we had another body to collect. Ten minutes later, Charlie and his po-faced friend trundled into the ward. This time, however, I did not manage to close all the other curtains, as I was halfway through turning one of the stroke patients and attending to his pressure areas by the time I realised that Charlie was on the ward. The evening visitors had also begun to arrive. The consequence of this was that Mr Barrie left the ward in his stainless steel trolley in full view of the patients and their visitors.

Meanwhile, as I stripped Mr Barrie's bed, I could hear the crash team talking: "Are we all agreed?" I dreaded those words. It indicated that the doctors had been unable to resuscitate Mr Dalkenny. Yet another life had come to an end. Sally came to help me make up Mr Barrie's bed. She looked pale and the dark rings under her eyes were developing rings of their own.

"Are you OK?" I asked her.

"I'll be all right," she said.

I couldn't say any more. I felt hot tears pricking at the back of my eyes. I had never imagined that a job, any job, could be quite like this.

As Sally and I cleaned up Mr Dalkenny's body and belongings, we heard the welcome sound of the arrival of the night shift. By the time we had finished, it was half an hour after our duty should have ended.

"Come home, ladies," said Staff Nurse Kerrigan, smiling now. Her hair was everywhere, and her starched cap was on a slant. "It's been a hell of a day."

Chapter Seventeen

At 7.30 the next morning, we were all back on duty for a repeat performance. The ward had been extremely busy overnight; almost as soon as a bed had become available, it had been filled by a new admission from Casualty.

As we walked on to the ward, it was obvious that the night staff had been run ragged. Two linen trollies filled to overflowing with dirty sheets and blankets stood just inside the double doors and as we walked on to the ward itself, all the patients were still in their beds.

Some of the men at the top end of the ward waved cheerily as we walked by. "Good morning, Nurses!" It was Mr Docherty, a middle-aged man with unstable diabetes. "Have you come back for more? We were worried that you might not come back again after last night!"

With that, he started to laugh loudly and Eddie joined in, only to go into one of his coughing spasms which left him puce and gasping for breath.

"Sorry, Eddie." Mr Docherty looked genuinely concerned. "I'll try to bear your chest in mind before I try cracking any more jokes."

But that was enough to start him giggling again and Eddie, whose colour had only just begun to return to normal, was off again.

At report, the night nurses explained that there had been four deaths and four admissions during that night. I was delegated to work at the bottom of the ward where there were three new admissions. Two of them were elderly stroke patients and one was a man with kidney disease. I braced myself for a hectic morning of washing and turning patients.

Mr Jenkins, the man with the kidney disease, had suffered with his condition for five years, but his symptoms had recently deteriorated. Consequently, he had been admitted to our ward for observation and assessment. His problems were caused by a diminishing blood supply to both of his kidneys. This had resulted from atherosclerosis, or narrowing of the renal arteries. One of the symptoms which Mr Jenkins had noticed was that he produced very little urine whilst he was up and about during the day, but within 20 minutes of lying down at night, the blood supply to his kidneys improved markedly and his bladder was full of urine. He would spend the next few hours going back and forth to empty his bladder.

This, obviously, was not giving him much opportunity to sleep very soundly and when I met him, Mr Jenkins looked exhausted.

"Good morning, Mr Jenkins!" I tried to sound bright and enthusiastic, but the jaundiced eye which opened from the bed looked less than impressed.

"It can't be time to get up yet, surely?" Both eyes were closed now and there was the hint of a snore about to issue from his tired face.

"I'm really sorry to bother you, but I must just check your blood pressure, not just once but twice." It was necessary to check the blood pressure in both arms to assess any discrepancy in blood supply to both sides of his body.

I rolled up the sleeve on his right arm and quickly took the reading: 150/90 mmhg, not too bad. On the left side, however, the readings were 170/110 mmhg – quite a discrepancy, but no different from his recordings on admission. Temperature and pulse rate were both normal, so I closed the curtains around his bed to block out the morning sunshine and suggested that he should try to get a little sleep before the doctors' round at nine o'clock.

Moving on to my next patient, I met Mr Selby, an 84-year-old gentleman who had suffered a minor stroke during the night. He was very agitated and confused by his new surroundings, in spite of having been given some sedation to help him sleep. "Where's Elsie? Where is she? Elsie! Elsie!" His frail voice was ringing down the ward.

"It's all right, Mr Selby. I'm here to help you. I'll look after you."

"I don't want you; I want Elsie!" Mr Selby was shouting now.

Sister put her head around the curtains. "Is everything all right in here, Nurse?"

"Mr Selby is calling for Elsie, Sister, and I don't think that I'm doing a very good job of calming him down."

Sister smiled at Mr Selby and then sat on his bed. "Now, now Harry, you don't need to worry. We're here to help you. You're in the Infirmary because you had a funny turn last night whilst you were at home, do you remember?"

"In the Infirmary? What the Dickens am I doing in the Infirmary? Only sick people go there and I've never had a day's sickness in my life. I've been abducted, that's what it is! Help! Help! Somebody get me out of here! They're holding me against my will! I'm a prisoner of war! It's the Japs! Oh my God, get me out of here!"

Harry Selby tried to manoeuvre himself out of bed, but the weakness in his arm and leg made his movements very difficult. Sister held his hand gently. "It's all right, Harry. We are here to help you." She was speaking slowly and calmly and stroking the old man's hand.

Harry turned his eyes to look into hers. "Who are you? What are you doing to me?"

Harry snatched his hand away from Sister and pulled the bedclothes up around his chin. "Help! Help! Somebody get me out of here!" For an elderly man, Harry was capable of producing a surprisingly strong voice.

Sister turned to me. "I think that we will need to speak to the house officer. Will you bleep him for me, Nurse?"

"Of course, Sister," and with that, I marched up to the top of the ward to make the call. I had to wait a couple of minutes for the doctor to return the call and, all the while, I could hear Harry's voice calling for help from the bottom of the ward. I could understand Harry's confusion and his fear. It must have been very frightening to experience a stroke and then to find himself transferred to a crowded ward in the middle of the night. He was separated from his family, his home and all that was familiar, so it was not surprising that he should feel this way.

The phone rang. "Ward 26. Student Nurse McIntosh speaking."

"You bleeped me?" It was a tired-sounding voice on the other end.

"Yes. I'm sorry to bother you, but we are having some trouble with one of the stroke patients admitted last night. He is very confused and we are having difficulty in calming him down."

"Didn't I prescribe some sedation during the night?" The voice was edged with irritation now.

"Yes, you did. This was administered by the night staff, but it is not showing any signs of being effective at the moment and it was written on his chart as a stat dose only, so we are unable to give anything else unless it is prescribed on the chart."

"Couldn't it wait until the doctors' round?"

"That is another hour to wait and I really don't think that it will benefit the patient to remain in this state for such a long time." I surprised myself by speaking so assertively.

"Very well. I'll be there as soon as I can." The phone clicked as he replaced the receiver. How long he would be was anyone's guess.

I walked quickly down the ward to Harry's bed. Sister was still with him and she was listening to one of his tales about life in the First World War. She turned slightly as I walked through the curtains. "Any luck?" she asked.

"He'll be here as soon as he can, Sister."

She raised her eyes heavenwards. "We could be here for the duration, then."

She turned to Harry. "Harry, I really need to get on with some of my jobs. The doctors are coming round in a little while and I really need to get things ready for them. Is it all right if I go and do that? Nurse McIntosh will sit with you and make sure that you are kept safe."

Harry looked doubtfully at me. "She's only a wee strip of a lass. How the Dickens is she going to look after me?"

Sister was beginning to look exasperated. "She may look that way, Harry, but she's perfectly capable of looking after you."

Harry took another look and, after a pause, conceded, "Very well, Sister, as long as you're sure."

"I'm sure, Harry. Don't you worry."

With that, Sister stood up slowly and, as she passed me, whispered, "He's all yours. Good luck!"

I resisted the rising sense of panic as I realised that I would now be unable to prepare all of my other patients for the doctors' round. I sat down where Sister had been sitting and began to ask Harry about himself and his experiences of life. Once into his stride, Harry was happy. As with many elderly people, his memory of events long ago was excellent. It was the recent past and the present which was causing him so much trouble.

Harry talked on about friends of his who had accompanied him to war and who had been killed in action. His face clouded with the memories of such things, so I tried to steer the conversation towards his family. This proved to be almost equally traumatic. Harry was the seventh and last child in his family. His father had been distant and austere and his mother had evidently struggled greatly to bring up her children. She died when Harry was only ten years old and it was at that time that Harry had been sent out to work, helping his father at the local dairy.

Half an hour later, Dr Sim popped his head around the curtains. "Mr Selby, I'm Dr Sim, I admitted you to the ward last night."

"Did ye? I cannae remember." Harry was beginning to look panicky again.

"Nurse here tells me that you've been feeling a bit anxious, is that right?"

"I dinna ken. I thought that I was all right. I thought that you were my Elsie." Harry turned to look accusingly at me. "You're not my Elsie! What are you doing sitting on my bed? Get off! Get away! I'll take my strap to ye!"

"It's all right, Harry." I tried to sound soothing but inwardly was beginning to feel that the situation was once again slipping out of my control. "Dr Sim is here to help you too."

"That's right, Harry. I just want to give you some medicine to help you feel more calm and to help you to get some rest. Is that OK?"

"I dinna want any o' your medicine, young man! For all I know, you could be about to poison me! Get away! Get away!"

"Mr Selby, you're in the Infirmary because you had a wee stroke during the night and you need us to help you to get better. Getting all het up is not going to help you now, is it?" Dr Sim was holding the medicine chart in his hand.

"I think we'll try some largactil intramuscularly and see how he goes with that." Dr Sim handed me the chart and hastily left the ward. I was left with the prospect of administering the injection to a man who was terrified of me even touching his hand, let alone plunging a needle into his buttock.

"Now, Harry, I'm just going to get this medicine for you. It will help you to feel better and you may even get the chance to have a little sleep. I'll only be a couple of minutes. OK?"

"OK, lass, whatever you say, as long as I can go home in a few minutes."

I smiled sweetly at Harry as I backed out of the curtains. Walking briskly up the ward, I tried to find Sister for the drugs keys so that I could draw up the prescribed injection. I found her frantically tidying the patients' files and placing each one in the appropriate part of the trolley in preparation for the round, which was due to commence in about five minutes.

We hastily checked and drew up the medication and I was about to ask Sister if she would accompany me to help calm Harry as I gave the injection, when the double doors opened and in walked one of the consultants with senior registrars, registrars, senior house officers, house officers and numerous medical students in his wake.

Sister marched up to the top of the ward with the files trolley and I went in the opposite direction in search of reinforcements. Unfortunately, everyone was very busy and I came to the conclusion that I would have to attempt the injection alone. With a compliant patient, this was no problem at all, but I had the strangest feeling that Harry was not going to fit into this category.

As I approached his bed, I could feel my palms sweating. I took a deep breath and, smiling, drew back the curtains. There, on the bed, lay Harry Selby. He was sound asleep. My prayers were answered. I would not need to give the injection after all. I checked that Harry's colour was good and that his breathing was clear and rhythmical. I backed out of the curtains, only to walk smartly into the bathing trolley, which had been left there by Sally, the junior student nurse.

The stainless steel basin hit the floor with a sound resembling one of Big Ben's chimes. Water splashed everywhere, particularly up the back of my legs, and soaked the back of my uniform. I held my breath, waiting for Harry to begin shouting for his Elsie once again, but there was silence behind the curtains.

I peeped through the gap to make sure that he was still breathing and, having reassured myself that he was fine, I set about mopping up the water which had been spilled. I also had to dispose of the medication in the syringe, as it was now no longer needed. On my quest in search of a mop, I had to sidle past the entourage which accompanied the consultant. I was attempting to keep my back away from their gaze, because I was still dripping slightly. I had almost made it past when Mr Docherty spoke out in one of his stage whispers: "Had a wee accident, Nurse?"

With that, the entire entourage turned in my direction and a smile flashed across the entire group faster than a Mexican wave. Sister's eyes rolled heavenwards and Eddie started coughing and wheezing once again. I could see that it was going to be one of those days.

Chapter Eighteen

By lunchtime, we were just about catching up with the bed baths, pressure area care, observations and drugs rounds. The ward was beginning to look more respectable, if somewhat full.

The lunch wagon arrived and Sally and I marched up and down the ward with the appropriate meals on trays for our patients. Some of the elderly gentlemen at the bottom of the ward were unable to feed themselves, so the auxiliaries, Sally and I sat down and assisted them.

I sat down gratefully next to Mr McCormack, a long-term patient on the ward. He was 96 years old and had suffered a stroke three months previously. He was very frail and spent most of his days either lying in his bed staring at the bay wall, or sitting in his armchair, staring into the middle distance.

"Lunchtime, Mr McCormack," I said, as enthusiastically as possible. "It looks very nice today; I hope that you will enjoy it."

I placed a napkin under his chin and prepared to mix the minced meat and mashed potatoes with the vegetables, which had already been puréed. I offered Mr McCormack a small taster on the spoon, but he turned his head away.

"It smells really good today. I'm sure you will enjoy it if you try a little bit." Again, he turned his head away.

I felt tired and hungry myself and I could feel the old impatience, born of fatigue, beginning to surface once again. I knew that it was important for all of the patients to eat in order to optimise health and I found it very difficult, after all the rushing about of the last 24 hours, to face this battle of wills.

I sat back and took a deep breath. I looked at Bev, Gladys and Sally, who were all successfully assisting their patients to eat. I felt tired, drained and defeated and, for a moment, wished that I could eat the meal myself. It was something that I would never do, but it was very tempting.

I put the spoon down and took hold of Freddy McCormack's hand. "Freddy, what's the matter?" I tried to sound gentle and prayed for more compassion, more patience, more love.

Freddy turned his face towards me and his eyes were full of tears. "I want to go home," he whispered. "Please let me go home."

"Oh, Freddy, I know you do, but you're not well enough to go home just yet."

He began to sob. I moved the tray of food away from him and took off the napkin. I reached across the bed to the box of tissues and gently wiped his eyes and helped him to blow his nose.

"I'm sorry, Nurse," he said, "but I cannae live like this any more. My family have all gone and I'm all alone in this ward full of noise and bustle. I'm 96, y' ken, and I'm just too tired to be doing with all o' this." Freddy's voice was hoarse with emotion.

I turned Freddy's face gently to look into his eyes. "Freddy, I know that you are tired of all this. It must be very difficult being here, seeing other people come and go, and I know that we are all so busy that we are not much company for you."

Freddy's eyes were beginning to brim with tears again. "It's just that I feel so useless here. I'm taking up a space that could be used by someone who wants to get better. What hope do I have? Look at me!" His last words were spat out with frustration, anger, loneliness and fear.

"You do matter, Freddy. You matter very much," I said.

"Do you really think so?" There was a hint of hope in his voice.

"I know so." I squeezed Freddy's hand gently and he began to smile. The tears began to roll down his face once again, but this time, they were tears of relief and not of anger. I helped Freddy to wipe his face once again and he turned to me and said, "Do you think you could do me a favour, Nurse?"

"I'll do my best, Freddy."

"Do you think you could give me ma lunch? I'm starving!"

True to his word, Freddy ate his lunch in double quick time and, as I settled him back on to his bed for an after-lunch nap, he looked much more peaceful and relaxed. I covered him over with a blanket and left him to rest. Sister called Sally and me away for our lunch and we gratefully headed for the canteen.

The morning had gone so quickly and it was bliss to sit down and have a rest for a while. The canteen was busy and filled with chat about the morning's adventures. Every few seconds, there was the sound of a bleep as a doctor was summoned away from an eagerly anticipated meal. It was interesting to watch the different ways in which doctors responded to their bleeps.

Some of the doctors merely glanced at the device attached to the pocket of their white coats, sat back and finished their meal, before sauntering out to the nearest phone to answer the call. Other, more junior, doctors would leap up, gulp down a mouthful of coffee and then rush out to the phones in the lobby outside the canteen. Occasionally, the crash team bleep would sound and the anaesthetist would leap up and literally run out of the room, his white coat streaming in his wake.

I was thankful that I was not carrying a bleep, and spent the half-hour break trying to recharge my failing batteries for the last three hours of the shift. I didn't feel much like talking; Sally had found some of the students in her set and was talking energetically with them. I sat looking into my coffee cup, for the millionth time pondering the meaning of life.

Before many minutes had passed, I realised that we were due back on the ward. I tapped Sally on the shoulder. "Time to go back, Sally."

She turned her weary face to me. "It can't be time yet, surely." Her tone was pleading.

"Never mind, it won't be long and let's face it, after last night and this morning, things can only get better."

But I was very wrong. As we returned to the ward, I could see the curtains had been drawn around Freddy's bed. The nurses' station was deserted. I put my handbag away quickly and had an awful feeling in my gut that something bad had happened.

With my heart in my throat, I gently parted the curtains and watched as Freddy's respirations ebbed and flowed. Whilst Sally and I had been away, Freddy had dramatically and fatally extended his stroke and he was in the process of dying. Freddy was NFR and at least he was able to die with peace and dignity. Sister turned to me as I entered the curtained area.

"Would you like to stay with him, Nurse McIntosh?" she whispered.

"Yes, Sister."

We swapped places and I sat on the bed and held Freddy's hand. Sister left the area and I gently stroked Freddy's face. "It's all right now, Freddy," I said. "You can rest now and nobody will be able to bother you any more."

Freddy sighed and then gently, almost imperceptibly, he passed quietly away. I sat with him for a few moments, holding his hand. I prayed silently that God would welcome Freddy into his Kingdom and I felt a great sense of peace. For the first time, I had been able to see death not as the great enemy, but as the reliever of suffering. I sat quietly embracing the peace for a moment longer and then, cradling Freddy's head in my arms, I laid him flat, and went to tell Sister that we needed the doctor to certify death.

"Very well," she said. "When the doctor has certified death, will you lay Freddy out, please?"

"Yes, Sister."

Dr Finnigan arrived about fifteen minutes later, still chewing on a sandwich. "You rang?" he smiled, half-heartedly.

"Yes, Mr McCormack has passed away and we need you to certify death, please."

"OK." Dr Finnigan followed me down to Freddy's cubicle. "He was definitely NFR, wasn't he?"

For a brief awful moment, I thought that perhaps we should have attempted resuscitation, but then common sense prevailed. "Yes, quite definitely. I'll fetch the notes for you from the trolley."

"Thanks." Dr Finnigan removed the stethoscope from around his neck and entered the curtained area. As I walked up the ward to the nurses' station, my mind reeled as it often did when it had reached overload. What if Freddy wasn't really dead at all? He might just be asleep. Just suppose that he woke up in the mortuary, encased in a shroud, in a refrigerated compartment. It was the stuff of nightmares and I inwardly told myself to get a grip.

I met Dr Finnigan outside Freddy's cubicle. "You're not wrong, you know," he said. "Dead as a dodo."

He took the notes from me and went to the desk to write up his findings. I was torn between laughing at his glib remarks and rebuking him for his apparent lack of respect. In the end, I decided that we all had our own ways of coping with the death of others, and said nothing.

I went to the linen cupboard to find another mortuary pack and, collecting the bathing trolley on the way back, set about preparing Freddy for his final journey out of the ward.

It took me about 20 minutes to complete the procedure, which I tried to perform with as much gentleness and respect as possible. I always tried to imagine that I was taking care of someone close to me, so that I would never perform this duty lightly or irreverently. When all was done, I telephoned the mortuary to let them know that there was a body to collect.

Charlie and his friend arrived about ten minutes later. Charlie was still as cheerful as ever and whistled as he rolled the stainless steel trolley down the ward. The patients on the other side of their closed curtains must have wondered why someone could be so happy about such a job as his. But Charlie was enigmatic. He was impossibly happy and, for this reason, he was exactly the right man for the job.

"The way I see it is this," he once told me. "We all come into the world and, one way or the other, we all have to leave it. I'm just helping people on their final journey."

The trolley rolled out of the ward and Sally and I pulled the curtains back from around the remaining patients.

"You're looking tired, Nurse." It was Mr Docherty. "Would you like to come and have a wee lie down wi' me?"

I blushed in response and said, "Thank you, Mr Docherty. I am tired, but not THAT tired."

He began to laugh and this, of course, set Eddie coughing and wheezing again. I went over to him as he was having real difficulty catching his breath. I increased the oxygen flow by another two litres per minute, as we had been instructed for Eddie when he experienced particularly bad episodes. I knelt by his chair and held his hand. Eddie was beginning to panic. I knew that he had just recently been given his lunchtime nebuliser, so I looked into his frightened eyes.

"Eddie, I want you to calm your breathing down. I need you to take a breath and then let it out . . . two . . . three, in . . . two . . . three, and out . . . two . . . three. That's it! Brilliant! Just keep concentrating on that rhythm and you will soon regain control."

Eddie struggled to keep the rhythm and his chest was sounding very rattly.

"Keep doing that, Eddie. You're doing really well. I'm just going to ask Sister to contact the doctor for you, because I think that you could do with a little extra help this time. But I'll be back in just a moment."

Eddie looked up from above his oxygen mask and his eyes were fearful and jaded. I squeezed his hand gently. "I'll be back in just a moment."

I shot off down the ward in search of Sister and found her writing up the nursing Kardex in preparation for the report when the afternoon shift were due to arrive.

"Sister, I'm sorry to bother you, but Eddie is having a particularly bad episode with his breathing. He has had his nebuliser, but I really think that he needs some extra assistance."

"I'll contact Dr Finnigan. You stay with Eddie and try to keep him calm."

With that, I walked briskly back to Eddie's bed. He was struggling to breathe and was using his shoulders in an attempt to allow more air to enter his lungs. He sounded very congested and was becoming much more cyanosed, on blue in colour, around his nose and the tips of his ears. His eyes were filled with fear and I could feel the knot in my stomach growing ominously. I always had this feeling when a patient's condition was deteriorating. I was beginning to feel Eddie's panic and was running out of ideas to help him.

"Just keep to the rhythm, Eddie; you're doing really well. The doctor will be here in a minute."

I kept repeating the rhythm like a mantra and found myself taking large gasps of air on Eddie's behalf, as if this would help him to breathe. After what seemed an age, Dr Finnigan returned to the ward.

"What is it about this place?" he grimaced as he saw Eddie's colour and his efforts to breathe. "What's the oxygen running at?"

"Six litres per minute."

"Increase it to eight. Eddie, I'm the doctor and I'm just going to listen to your chest. You're having a wee bit of difficulty with your breathing?"

Eddie nodded frantically. Dr Finnigan listened to Eddie's chest. "He sounds as if he's full of fluid. I'll prescribe some frusemide." He wrote out the chart quickly. "Draw that up, stat."

Taking the chart immediately, I grabbed Staff Nurse Kerrigan and asked her to check the medication with me. It had been written up as an intravenous medication and Dr Finnigan had said that he would stay with Eddie whilst I was preparing it.

My hands were shaking as I drew up the drug. I held the syringe upright and removed the last little air bubble from it. A small drop of fluid spurted out of the needle. I hastily double-checked the drugs chart and countersigned the document, then took the syringe to Dr Finnigan, who was sitting by Eddie, attempting to insert a Venflon into his right arm.

"His veins are shutting down. I'm having a hell of a job to find a decent one," he muttered under his breath.

I knelt by Eddie's left side and held his hand. "It won't be long now, Eddie, and we'll be able to give you this medicine which should help you to feel a lot better."

Eddie was wincing with the pain of the Venflon, which Dr Finnigan was probing into his arm. Once inserted, the Venflon would give us instant access to a vein, should any further intravenous drugs need to be administered. It seemed an age before Dr Finnigan triumphantly straightened up, saying, "Bullseye!"

The dark red blood which leaked from the Venflon indicated that a vein had been reached. I quickly taped the Venflon into position. Dr Finnigan checked the ampoule of frusemide and carefully administered the drug. "This will help to get rid of the fluid on your lungs, Eddie." He turned to me: "Has he been catheterised?"

Remembering my first encounter with Eddie and the urinal, I was able to inform Dr Finnigan that he definitely was not.

"I think that Eddie would be better catheterised because, once this frusemide begins to take effect, he is likely to be producing a great deal of urine."

"I'll set up a trolley."

As I marched off up the ward to the procedures room, Dr Finnigan spoke into Eddie's ear. "Eddie, we're just going to put a wee tube into your bladder. It's going to help drain away all the pee that's going to come away after this injection."

Eddie nodded. He was still unable to speak. I think that he may have been bemused by the idea that an injection in his arm was going to help with his breathing, but that it necessitated a tube going into his bladder. He was not in a position to ask too many questions about it and a couple of minutes later, I was drawing the curtains around his bed and assisting him to lie down on it.

I helped to undress Eddie as discreetly as possible and then poured out the antiseptic and the lignocaine gel, and finally opened the sterile urinary catheter on to the trolley. Dr Finnigan was very adept and managed to insert the catheter quickly and with as little trauma as possible. I drew up ten millilitres of sterile water with which to inflate the balloon which would keep the catheter in place and then attached a catheter bag, which would hang on a hook discreetly at the side of Eddie's bed.

The bag was already beginning to fill and, within a few minutes, Eddie was beginning to breathe a little more easily. I cleared the rubbish away from the trolley and Dr Finnigan stayed with Eddie for a few more minutes, to listen to his chest and ensure that this was all that was needed at the present time.

"I turned the oxygen back down to six litres and he seems to be tolerating this quite well. Keep him on this for another couple of hours and then return it to four litres per minute."

Turning to Eddie, Dr Finnigan said, "I think that this should help, Eddie. I've told Nurse here to keep a good eye on you and not to give you too much trouble."

Eddie smiled. His face was relaxing and his colour was definitely improving. I felt relieved. As I pulled back the curtains surrounding Eddie's bed, I saw the anxious face of Mr Docherty.

"Is Eddie all right, Nurse? I shouldn't have made him laugh; it's all my fault." He looked quite crestfallen.

"Eddie is a lot better now. Please don't feel that it was your fault. It's people like you who keep us going."

Mr Docherty smiled. "And it's nurses like you who get us going." He started to laugh again and all the men in the bay, including Eddie, joined in.

Chapter Nineteen

A few days later, a letter arrived in my pigeonhole at the post office. It looked official and, as always with such envelopes, my heart skipped a beat. Opening it, I found a small memo inside which simply read:

Dear Miss McIntosh,
  It has come to our attention that you will shortly finish your nursing training and will be required to attend for an interview concerning your future deployment within this hospital. Please contact Sister on extension 0023 to arrange an interview.
  Yours sincerely,
  Chief Nursing Officer

I groaned inwardly. Yet another hurdle to overcome. I had already been making tentative moves towards a post in the Oral Surgery Department. I had decided that if I was to achieve my goal of obtaining the Pelican badge, which was awarded after training at the Infirmary and then completing one year's post-registration experience as a staff nurse, then I would like to obtain roughly half of it in surgical, and the other half in medical nursing.

My palms were sweating as I dialled the nursing officer's office. These life-changing moments always left me with an outbreak of desperate butterflies in the pit of my stomach. The phone was answered quickly: "Nursing officers."

I took a deep breath and, as usual, a squeaky voice escaped from my tight throat. "Good morning. Yes, I would like to make an appointment concerning a post as a staff nurse in the Oral Surgery Department, please."

"Are you a student nurse at the present time?" The voice sounded bored, yet incisive at the same time.

"Yes, I am. I have just received a memo from you, or your office, this morning. My training is due to finish in two weeks' time." I felt myself beginning to falter. "And I would very much like to complete a year's work here as a staff nurse, if at all possible."

I cringed as the words crawled on their hands and knees down the phone to the woman sitting upright, and no doubt immaculately, on the other end.

"What is your name?" she sighed as she reached for the diary. I told her and she arranged an interview for ten o'clock the following morning. I explained that I had hoped to work in the Oral Surgery Department, but I was not sure that she was paying much attention. She gave the impression that she had far more interesting things to do with her time than to sit answering the phone.

Next morning, I gave my black shoes an extra polish and made sure that the third-year nursing cap was exactly straight, took a deep breath, and found myself at the polished oak door once again. I tried to make my knock sound confident, but some of its verve was lost between the intention and the actual delivery. I waited, but nothing happened. I knocked again, this time convincing my hand that it really needed to make contact with the door in order to do any good. Success.

"Come!" I do wish that people would not say that. It sounds so officious, the sort of tone that one uses with a dog. I came to the conclusion that there were so many ways in which some people established their authority over others. I wondered why it was so necessary. The people I respected the most were those who were willing to get their hands dirty, who obviously knew what it was like to struggle and yet to overcome.

I walked into the office, once more taken aback by the austerity of the polished oak. Two nursing officers sat on the opposite side of the desk.

"Nurse McIntosh, do sit down."

I felt like a poodle. If they had told me to stand up and beg, I probably would have given it a try. I hated the effect these people had on me. I smiled and folded my hands in my lap. The image of the poodle remained unnervingly clear in my mind's eye.

"We understand that you would like to take up a post in the Oral Surgery Department. Is that right?"

"Yes, that's right. I understand that a position is already available there. Is that correct?"

"Yes, it is. We have seen from your training records that after a shaky start, you seem to have done rather well."

A flicker of a smile crossed the face of the nursing officer who was speaking. I couldn't be sure whether it was a genuine reflection of human warmth, or the sort of smile which appears on the face of psychopaths in all the horror movies. I decided not to let my guard down, just in case.

"Are you intending to work for long in the unit?" This was a tricky one. I decided that honesty was the best policy and explained that my goal at present was to work for a year as a staff nurse, splitting the time between surgical and medical nursing. The nursing officers looked at each other. I couldn't tell if this was a positive look, or a "Don't touch her with a barge pole" look.

"So, basically, you intend to stay for your Pelican and then leave?"

I felt anxious. What should I say? If I said "Yes", they might assume that I was not committed. If I said "No", then they might wonder why I only wanted to work in the department for six months.

"I do want to receive my Pelican badge," I said. "But after that, I am not sure. I have been considering the possibility of going on to train as a midwife. I want to keep my options open at the moment."

The nursing officers looked at each other again. "Would you mind leaving us for a few moments, Nurse?"

"Yes. Yes, of course." I stood up quickly and subdued the instinct to bow or curtsy. I turned towards the door and my hand slipped on the brass doorknob because it was so wet.

I sat dejectedly in the waiting area and anxiously nibbled on the few remaining shreds of fingernails which were left. My stomach was in danger of returning the morning offering of breakfast. "Oh Lord, why do I keep putting myself through one ordeal after another? I must be mad. There surely is a better way to go about earning a living than this?"

There wasn't time to hear an answer. The huge door swung open and I was ushered back inside. "We have considered your application and have decided to offer you the post, starting in two weeks' time."

"Thank you. Thank you so much." For some reason, I was elated. I had just secured a further period of my life under the auspices of these terrifying women and there I was, thanking them so profusely. There are times when I seriously wonder about the sanity of it all.

I left the office and walked quickly back to the nurses' home. I removed my uniform with some difficulty, as it was clinging to my sodden back. I flopped on the bed, closed my eyes and thanked God that at least the way forward had become a little clearer.

The remaining two weeks of training continued in much the same vein as the previous 154. It was hectic, exhausting and, at times, heart-rending. I began to feel a certain detachment creeping over me as, one by one, the shifts began to count down to the final day as a student nurse.

I noticed that I began to pour myself out less with my patients and, at the end of each shift, just felt glad to have survived, and hoped that I had done enough to help people when they needed it the most. With my goal in sight, I suddenly seemed overwhelmed by fatigue and, instead of feeling elation, as I had anticipated, I only felt tired and flat and dispirited.

I decided that a visit to Ted and Helen was required. Ted and Helen were an elderly couple from the Chapel who were no longer able to attend church on a regular basis, but who had opened their hearts and their home to me when I arrived in Edinburgh. I had visited them regularly throughout my training and had found great comfort and solace in their little two-up two-down home, which was filled with trinkets and nick-nacks from many years gone by.

I telephoned and arranged to visit them on the Wednesday afternoon. I took, as always, a large bag of fresh fruit to replenish their fruit bowl and, after walking the two and a half miles to their home, I was soon sitting down, drinking tea from a bone china teacup.

"How's it going, Hilary?" Helen, as always, put other people's concerns before her own.

"I am due to finish my training next week."

"Oh, that's wonderful news, Hilary." Helen turned to face Ted and, raising her voice slightly, said, "Did you hear that, Ted? Hilary's nearly finished her training!"

"Oh, that's marvellous! It only seems a wee minute since you first walked in that door and now you're a fully fledged staff nurse. What a marvellous answer to prayer!"

I felt thoroughly ashamed, as I suddenly realised how very much Ted and Helen had supported me through the three years. Their prayers had been pivotal in whether I would stay the course, or not.

Ted was talking again. "You know how much we think of nurses, don't you? When Helen was ill five years ago, with the breast cancer, the nurses at the Infirmary looked after her so well and brought her back from death's door. We'll never forget the love and care they showed her. You nurses are such wonderful people."

I felt a prick of conscience when I thought about my attitude towards my work over the past week.

"We are only people, Ted," I said, "and we do make mistakes and find it difficult to be kind to everyone, all the time."

"Oh, aye, Hilary, I ken that, but it takes a special sort of person who can care for others and cope with the amount of work that you nurses do. I've sat on the ward watching the nurses rushing up and down, fetching and carrying, hour after hour, and yet having time for a kind word for everyone. Nursing is a calling, Hilary. There's no two ways about it."

If it was a calling, I wondered, why did I feel so empty as I stood on the brink of achieving my life's ambition? I smiled at Ted and thanked him for his wonderful support and affirmation.

Helen announced that tea was ready. As usual, she had prepared a wonderful feast of Scottish scones with strawberry jam, and numerous cakes and chocolate biscuits. She had prepared enough to feed a small regiment.

"Let's just thank the Lord for all that he has done for us." Ted said grace and then handed me a beautiful bone china plate – the best one on the table.

"Do tuck in," he said. "I expect you're hungry."

Somehow, between the scone and the final chocolate finger, I felt that my sadness had gone. In its place I felt a rising sense of hope. It was as though, just by being with Ted and Helen in their lovely little home, my batteries had been recharged and I had been given the boost I needed to finish the final lap of the course.

Neither Ted nor Helen were Bible-bashers; they just simply lived their faith. They were not embarrassed to talk about Jesus and referred to him with reverence but also familiarity, as one would with a special family member. They had known many sadnesses in their lives. They had never been able to have children of their own, but, instead of becoming bitter and angry with God, they had turned their love and affection outwards, to embrace many who needed their special brand of love and wisdom. Ted and Helen were an inspiration.

As the evening came to an end, Ted put on his hat and coat. "I'll walk you to the bus," he said.

"Oh, no, Ted, it's OK; I'll walk home."

"It's too dark for you to walk all that way on your own, Hilary. I'm taking you to the bus." It was this fatherlike care and concern which meant so much. I kissed Helen goodbye and then walked, arm in arm with Ted, all the way to the bus stop.

On the way, Ted told me about a worrying development with Helen's health. She had been developing persistent back pains, which were becoming more and more difficult to disguise with painkillers.

"I ken that she didn't show that she was in pain today, but when the tablets wear off, she's in an awfy state." I felt a stab of guilt that I hadn't even noticed.

"Will she see your doctor, Ted?"

"You ken what she's like. I have an awfy job getting her to do anything concerning her own health. I think that spell in the Infirmary has frightened her more than a wee bitty and she feels that if she doesn't say anything to the GP then it will all go away."

"She must see a doctor, Ted. Do all you can to persuade her. Would it help if I wrote a little note along those lines?"

The bus appeared around the corner. "Aye, it might." He looked doubtful. The bus was at the stop. "On you get, Hilary. I hope that we'll be seeing you again in a wee while."

I kissed Ted on his cheek. "Thank you so much for a lovely evening, and thank you for your prayers – they mean so very much."

I climbed on to the bus and we moved quickly up the hill. Ted was still waving as we rounded the bend at the top of the hill and swung around the corner, out of sight.

Chapter Twenty

Next morning, as I was checking the post, I discovered another official brown envelope amongst the five airmail letters from home. The airmail deliveries seemed to work on the same principle as the buses in Britain. You wait ages for one and then several come all at once. I filed the light blue airmail letters in date order and looked forward to reading through them over a cup of coffee, back in my room.

Walking quickly, I opened the brown envelope. Inside was an invitation to attend for measurement for my staff nurse's uniform. My stomach somersaulted. Yes! I was finally going to look the part and have a starched white cap with a royal blue ribbon, which was to be my badge of office.

I read through the letters from home and, as usual, Mum had managed to convey a great deal of love and encouragement. I missed her so much and found it difficult to think of the thousands of miles which separated us. I wished that she could be here today, when I would try on the new uniform for the first time. I sighed as I left my room and headed out into the sunshine and across the quadrangle to the warren of offices which housed everything from CSSD, the Central Sterile Supplies Department where all the surgical instruments were cleaned and sterilised, to the dressmaking department.

I rang the bell and, after a while, a very short and rotund woman wearing a tape measure around her neck, much in the way that doctors wear a stethoscope, came to open the door.

"Follow me," she said and I walked slightly behind her, as the corridor was not wide enough to accommodate both of us. I was almost lulled into a stupor by her metronomic movement from side to side.

"It's a staff nurse's uniform; is that right, hen?"

"That's right. I'm really looking forward to this."

She gave me a sideways glance. I suddenly thought that she meant that I was looking forward to having my body touched by a complete stranger. I blushed at the very thought and stammered, "I mean, I am really looking forward to becoming a staff nurse."

"Oh, aye," she said, but her face held the expression, "Don't bother."

The measuring went quite well and I was soon making a return journey down the corridor and back into the sunshine. I suddenly realised that I hadn't checked when I could collect the uniforms and went rushing back to the sewing room.

"Och, that was quick." There was almost a smile on her world-weary face.

"When will the uniforms be ready, please?"

"Och, it will take about four days. You can come and collect them then."

"Thank you very much."

"Close the door on your way out."

I turned around and left the dark and stuffy room, and followed the pipes which ran along the ceiling. They looked as though they had seen better days. Paint was peeling off them, as a result of transporting thousands of gallons of hot water over the years.

I blinked in the strong sunlight as I opened the external door. It was lovely to feel the fresh air again. Only five more shifts to go, and then I would be free. Well, almost.

One o'clock came and, once again, I was taking report at the nurses' station, in preparation for the evening shift. The ward was busy and bustling as the auxiliaries tidied away the lunch trays from each of the beds and attended to the needs of the patients. As I had walked on to the ward, I was vaguely aware that something was wrong. There was someone missing.

Sister was looking tired and a strand of her usually immaculate hair was dangling in front of her eyes as she rapidly completed the nursing Kardex before we sat down.

"It's been an awful morning," she whispered. "Eddie Burney developed severe breathing difficulties and there was nothing we could do to help him. He arrested before Dr Finnigan could get here and he was gone before the crash team arrived. The others in the bay are very upset. I've had to contact their relatives and have said that they can come in early for visiting this afternoon to try to comfort them."

I felt as though a lead weight had dropped to the pit of my stomach. Eddie had been a real character and had struggled hard to cope with his disabling chronic bronchitis. He had been part of the fabric of the ward, by adding his own character, his views, and his complaints. I had come to think of Ward 26 almost as Eddie Burney's ward. Ever since the time when he had experienced that acute episode of difficulty with his breathing and had pulled through, I had thought that he would just live on and on.

I felt as though I had just lost a friend and I knew that I would not be given the space, nor the time, to grieve for him. Not yet, anyway.

Staff Nurse Booth and Staff Nurse Kierney looked at each other. "It's going to be one of those evenings." We were on take again and Sister had done her best to ensure that as many patients who were well enough to be discharged had been so, to ensure that we had as many beds as possible free to admit patients from Accident and Emergency later in the day.

It was rare to have any spare beds on the ward, and it wasn't long before the Casualty senior house officer was ringing to say that there was a new admission for us, a 58-year-old man with chest pain. CCU was full and we were the only medical ward with any room to accommodate him.

I collected all the appropriate charts, name tags and paraphernalia necessary to document his admission and was just turning the bed back when his trolley was wheeled on to the ward. Unusually, the senior house officer had accompanied the patient and was looking anxious as the trolley was swung into position next to the waiting bed.

"This is Mr Dalgetty. He developed pains in his chest at half past twelve this afternoon and his wife called an ambulance shortly afterwards. As you can see, he is having some difficulty with his breathing and I am rather concerned about his colour. CCU is full and the ECG showed no changes as yet, so we're assuming that the pain is more pulmonary than cardiac. He has been on six litres of oxygen since admission. He has not lost consciousness but is obviously anxious, dyspnoeic and in pain. We have contacted the Scan Department to arrange an emergency thoracic scan, but the scanner is down at the moment. We have decided to initiate thrombolytic therapy, making the assumption from the history of sudden onset of pain and dyspnoea that we could be dealing with a pulmonary embolism."

I handed the doctor the medicine chart so that he could prescribe the required analgesia and thrombolytic therapy. I checked that the IVI was patent and running smoothly. It was going to be vital that we had instant access to a vein, should Mr Dalgetty's condition deteriorate, so that the necessary drugs could be administered immediately.

"Mr Dalgetty, welcome to Ward 26. Let me help you across from the trolley and into your bed."

The two porters, the SHO, Mrs Dalgetty and I all helped him to slide across. I made an "armchair" with the pillows, to help him to sit as upright as possible in bed, to facilitate his breathing. He was very breathless and he was sweating profusely, yet his skin was cold and clammy to the touch.

"Let me just check your blood pressure." My hands were shaking as I quickly wrapped the cuff around his arm. I could feel his condition deteriorate second by second. I inflated the cuff and placed the end of the stethoscope over the brachial artery. The blood pressure was only just audible at 90/50 – he was going into shock.

Mr Dalgetty grasped at the oxygen mask on his face. "Help me, please help me. I don't want to die."

"It's OK, Mr Dalgetty. We're here to help you." But, just as I said the words, he convulsed. The clot which was occluding part of his lung had moved suddenly and had occluded the coronary arteries. He had arrested.

I heaved off the bedhead and removed the pillows and, as I lowered Mr Dalgetty's head, his feet shot up in the air because of the convulsion. A jug of water was sent smashing to the floor.

Sister came shooting in behind the curtains. "What on earth is going on here?" She took one look and turned on her heel. "I'll call the crash team."

The SHO and I attempted CPR and continued until the rumble of the crash trolley announced the arrival of the team. We then handed over to them, but I think that we all knew that it was hopeless. Meanwhile, Mrs Dalgetty had been standing, watching, hoping and praying. I felt ashamed as I realised that none of us had even noticed that she was there.

I touched her gently on her arm. "Mrs Dalgetty, would you like to come with me? Perhaps you would like to come and sit in the relatives' room?"

She stood completely motionless, hardly breathing. Her eyes were wide open and her left hand covered her mouth. A single tear appeared and ran slowly down her left cheek. I tried again, this time with a little more urgency. I didn't want her to see the desperate efforts being made on the bed in front of her eyes.

"No," she whispered. "I want to stay here. He needs me

here." I felt terrible. Her husband would not need her anymore. He would not need another person again.

I placed my arm around her shoulder and rubbed her arm gently. Beneath my hands I felt the first surge of angry, disbelieving grief erupt from the very core of her being. Her sobs were terrible. I didn't know what to do, so I held her gently, rubbing her shoulders and saying, "It's all right, it's all right." It was anything but all right.

One of the doctors turned to look at Mrs Dalgetty for the first time. He looked angrily at me. "Get her out of here, Nurse."

"Mrs Dalgetty would prefer to stay." I tried to sound as though I was in control of the situation. The sobbing continued, coming in great waves which left her shaking. Suddenly, her knees gave way. I just managed to support her and swing her around to an armchair which was fortuitously near the foot of the bed.

Sister had witnessed the situation and she came quickly to my side. "She's fainted. Quickly, Nurse, get her head down. Lay her on the floor and elevate her feet."

Together we managed the manoeuvre, and Mrs Dalgetty quickly regained consciousness. For one moment she looked at us with relief, as though she felt that she was waking from a nightmare. When she realised who we were, and where she was, she rolled on her side and sobbed uncontrollably once again.

"Get the screens and a blanket, Nurse. This is hardly helping the other patients on the ward."

I rushed to wheel the mobile screens into position and carried back a blanket and a pillow for Mrs Dalgetty.

Behind the curtains, the crash team had decided that the fight was futile and that their patient was indeed dead. They collected their trolley and restocked it quickly with syringes and needles from our ward. One of the doctors put his head around the screen. He beckoned to me to come and speak with him. I followed him outside. "We've not been successful, I'm afraid. Do you think that Mrs Dalgetty is up to hearing the news yet?"

"I think that she already knows the outcome," I said, "but I will stay with her when you speak with her."

"OK."

Together, we went back behind the screen. Mrs Dalgetty was quiet now. She was sitting up, hugging her knees, and rocking gently back and forth. The doctor knelt down beside her. "Mrs Dalgetty, I'm sorry that we have not been able to save your husband. We did all that we could, but his condition was just too severe."

She turned to look at him. "I know," she whispered. "He was everything to me. Thank you for doing all you did." She struggled bravely to control the tears.

The doctor smiled gently and then said, "I will send another doctor to complete all the forms for you." At that moment, his emergency bleep sounded, and he leapt to his feet, and headed off to his next assignment.

"Would you like a cup of tea, Mrs Dalgetty?" I was trying to do something, anything that might be helpful.

"I'd love one, Nurse. Thank you."

"Let me take you to the relatives' room now. I'll bring you some tea and then, in a little while, we can see your husband again, together. Is that OK?"

She nodded sadly. I helped her up slowly and smoothed her skirt and cardigan which had become crumpled on the floor. I rolled the screen aside and gently led her up the ward to a small side-room where she could have some privacy. She seemed exhausted – too tired to care whether the patients on the ward were looking at her or not. I kept my arm around her and guided her to the room. She chose a chair near to the door and sat down heavily. I moved the box of paper handkerchiefs on to the coffee table next to her chair.

"I'll get you that cup of tea now. Would you like sugar?"

She shook her head. "Graham would like sugar though"

– and then she suddenly realised that Graham was not in need of a cup of tea, because he was dead. "Oh, God" she said, "Oh, God, oh, God."

I knelt beside her chair and gently stroked her hand. I couldn't think of anything helpful to say. I wanted to say, "God does know what you are going through and he cares so much about you", but I felt that the words would sound hollow and unreal somehow. I just kept stroking her hand and prayed for her silently.

After a few minutes, peace seemed to return and I left Mrs Dalgetty in order to make her cup of tea. Outside the relatives' room, Sister was waiting for me.

"What have you been doing in there, Nurse? There's a ward full of ill people who need your care. You can't spend the entire shift looking after one relative."

"I know that, Sister, but Mrs Dalgetty needed someone with her for a little while and I am just going to get her a cup of tea."

"When you've done that, come and lay out the body."

"Yes, Sister."

I returned to the room with the tea and explained to Mrs Dalgetty that I would be back in about 20 minutes.

I gathered the bathing trolley and a shroud pack and headed off to where Mr Dalgetty lay. One of the doctors had covered him with a sheet and when I pulled this back, his cold, battered body lay silently on the bed. A small trickle of blood lay drying on one side of his mouth, and his lips were purple. I thought back to his last words, "I don't want to die", and shivered.

An overwhelming sense of sadness came over me as I worked to prepare his body for the mortuary. This man had been well this morning. He had got up, eaten his breakfast, had a wash, got dressed – all the things that we all do as a matter of course. Little did he know that his life would be over by lunchtime.

Sudden death is so traumatic. I wondered how the souls

of such people are cared for after death. My Christian faith teaches that death is not the end, but a movement forward to eternal life. As I looked at the empty shell which lay on the bed in front of me now, I had to believe that this was true. There had to be something more. The human spirit is too precious a thing to be snuffed out completely.

I combed Mr Dalgetty's hair and covered him with the gown. When I had finished, I brought his wife in to see him. She hesitated at the curtain and then walked slowly towards him – the man she had loved and shared her life with for the past 33 years. She walked up to the bed slowly and picked up his hand.

"Oh, Graham, why did you have to leave me? Couldn't you have stayed just a wee while longer? There was so much that I wanted to tell you, so much that I wanted you to know."

I placed a chair next to where she was standing. "Stay a while," I said. I left them together. At least one of them would be able to say their goodbyes.

The rest of the ward continued on its busy way: buzzers ringing, the drugs trolley rolling down the ward, the mobile blood pressure machine rattling on one of its dodgy wheels as it was moved from patient to patient; the sound of the early shift saying farewell to the patients as they walked out of the ward; the sound of someone coughing productively and the bedpan washer swooshing and gurgling as it dealt with yet another offering.

I was busy checking the urine samples of the diabetics and writing up the results on the appropriate charts, when Mrs Dalgetty emerged from the curtains. She looked exhausted, but at the same time, she looked at peace.

"Would you like me to contact someone to come and take you home?"

"No, thank you, Nurse. There is nobody who can help. I've got to accept the fact that I'm on my own now."

"Will you be all right?"

"I'll have to be." She smiled bravely. "I only live a wee while away and I'll walk home. The dogs will be wondering where we – I've got to. Thank you for all your help."

"I'm so sorry that we couldn't do any more."

"At least I know that everything was done that could have been done. Please tell the doctor that I will come back tomorrow for the papers he said I would need." I was amazed at her composure. With that, she walked purposefully out the ward.

I completed last offices and contacted the mortuary. Ten minutes later, Charlie and his friend came whistling down the ward. "You're doing a roaring trade again today, Nurse." Charlie winked as he swung the steel trolley next to the bed.

"When you're ready, Sam . . . One, two, three." With that, Mr Dalgetty's body was lifted into the trolley and wheeled on its way out of the ward.

You had to be a certain sort of person to do a job like that.

Chapter Twenty-One

I couldn't believe it. The young woman standing facing me in the mirror, wearing a starched white uniform and cap, and sporting a pair of lily-white shoes, was me. The cap flopped and wobbled somewhat as I practised moving and talking. This was going to need some more starch, or people might mistake the head gear for an animate object of some description.

I still had another 24 hours in which to sculpt the object into the required shape, before I commenced duty for the first time as a staff nurse. I changed out of the dress and headed off for the laundry room, armed with a new packet of spray starch. On the way, I met Shahida. "I was just coming to see you," she said.

"I'm just trying to starch this hat into some sort of order. Do you want to come and talk while I beat it into submission?"

Shahida sat on a three-legged stool in the laundry room whilst I ironed the hat repeatedly. The problem was that I had used so much starch that the hat no longer looked white. The starch seemed to attract nasty black smears and I was beginning to think that I was fighting a losing battle with it.

"Oh! What am I going to do with this?" I was getting exasperated now. Shahida smiled patiently.

"It looks OK, Hil. Don't worry about it. I wish that this was all I had to worry about."

"What's the matter, Shahida?"

"Last night, when I was on night duty, an elderly man

passed away. The problem was that when I went to check him on a routine ward round, he still had a weak pulse. It was only very weak and he was gently passing away. I knew that his prognosis was very poor, so I didn't initiate CPR but called the SHO instead. By the time he arrived, the patient had died, and I have been reported to the powers that be. I'm going to have to give a statement to the police about it and I don't know if this is going to stop me from qualifying in six weeks' time."

"Oh, Shahida, that's terrible! They can't do that to you. You are a born nurse. You were only acting in the best interests of your patient. As you say, he was dying anyway. How would bouncing up and down on his chest and ramming tubes down his throat have made his death more dignified or peaceful?"

"I know, I know. I took the decision because I wanted him to be spared all that pain and humiliation. The problem is that I'm not qualified – yet – and a student nurse should not make such decisions."

"Well, perhaps someone should have thought of that before they decided that it was OK to leave us in charge of so many people."

I felt angry and indignant that Shahida should have been put in this impossible position. I felt that she had made the right decision for her patient and was not sure that I would have had the same courage had I been in her place.

"Come on," I said. "Let's go out to lunch at Hendersons."

Out in the sunshine, the world seemed a better place, but Shahida still looked tired and pale.

"This night duty is really getting me down," she said. "I feel as though I am just going through the motions now. I've passed my exams, but I am not considered qualified. Where does this leave us?"

It was unlike Shahida to be so despondent.

"Well, at least you've got a holiday coming up now,

Shahida. Are you still sure that you want me to look after Ruby for you?"

Shahida smiled. "I'm sure if you're sure."

"Of course I'm sure. After all, how much trouble can one little hamster be?"

Later that afternoon, Shahida and Ruby made their clandestine journey to my room and Shahida gave me strict instructions about cleaning the cage regularly and not forgetting to feed Ruby on a daily basis. I manoeuvred the cage into the bottom of my wardrobe and made sure that none of the clothes came into contact with it. I didn't fancy the idea of chewed hemlines.

Shahida gave Ruby one last cuddle and then she set off to pack her things in readiness for her holiday. She had recently bought herself a second-hand Ford Fiesta, which she had laughingly nicknamed "the Rocket". She threw all her bags in the back and set off for Manchester, where she was going to have some rest at home with her family.

I was sad to see her go. Shahida had become my best friend, someone I could always count on to be kind, patient and understanding, and also blessed with a zany sense of humour. At least I had her hamster for company.

The next morning, I was pacing my room in readiness for my first shift as a staff nurse. The time seemed to pass so slowly and I really didn't know what to do with myself as I waited for the afternoon to begin. I spent some time talking to Ruby's cage. I would have talked to Ruby herself, but she could not be seen amongst all the bedding in the top chamber. I checked all the locks were secure on the cage, to make sure that she had not made a bid for freedom when I hadn't been paying attention. No, they were all OK; she must just be sleeping.

The clock ticked on. It was half past ten and I could bear being inside no longer, so I decided to go out for a walk. Heading down the Mound, I suddenly had a brainwave and decided to have my hair cut. I rushed into the nearby salon and asked if someone could cut my hair NOW. The receptionist checked the book and said that that was possible. Would I like to take a seat?

My hair was washed by a young woman with attitude. I tried not to wince as she roughly pulled my hair and pushed my head around in the basin as though it was a cabbage. The temperature of the water suggested that she had nerves of steel in her hands. When I opened my eyes it was difficult to see through the haze of steam. Wrapping a towel roughly around my head, she pointed to a seat in front of an old mirror. "Sit there, hen."

I obediently sat down. I should have taken a hint and walked straight out of the door, but like an idiot, I meekly did as I was told, hoping against hope that the haircut would surpass the treatment thus far.

The hairdresser herself emerged from behind a beaded curtain, still smoking a cigarette. Her hands were huge and she breathed heavily as she moved around in the confined space of the salon. She set to with her comb and scissors. I didn't realize until later that she didn't even ask me what I would like my hair to look like at the end of all this. I had taken off my glasses and couldn't clearly see what she was doing as she prodded my head from side to side and snipped away with frightening speed.

After about five minutes, she spoke up. "Will that do yer?"

I put on my glasses and, to my horror, the hair which had once been shoulder length was now in an uneven bob, with one side a good couple of centimetres shorter than the other. The fringe was also on a slant.

"It'll be OK when you dry it, hen" she said. "That will be £4.50."

In a daze, I looked in my purse and paid the required amount. A little voice at the back of my mind was protesting for all it was worth. "You're not going to actually pay her for this, are you? You look like a scarecrow."

Alarmingly, I heard my own voice thanking the woman

for her time and even leaving a tip. I left the salon and decided to go back to the nurses' home to try and make my hair look presentable. I was angry with myself for being so weak. I should have complained, but had been too afraid to create a scene. When would I ever learn?

It was quite difficult to create a tidy hairstyle, but I did my best and had to resort to using my nursing scissors to even up the disaster. Finally, I was dressed and ready to face the world in my new role. I was terrified.

My hands were shaking as I locked the door to my room and strode down the corridor, attempting to look calm and serene. The image was marred somewhat by my tripping over a door wedge at the far end. These new shoes would take some getting used to.

Out into the sunshine and the knot in my stomach had grown to the size of a football. In through the double doors and the familiar smells and sounds of the hospital partially calmed me and also made me feel like a horse which has only recently been broken – in submission to its master.

Turning right down the corridor, I smiled at Charlie as he and his comrade trundled a body away from Ward 31. "Hello, Nurse!" Charlie called, smiling as usual. "You're looking very grand today."

"Thank you, Charlie, but I'm terrified."

"First day in the whites?"

I nodded. "Och, you'll be fine, Nurse; you just wait and see." With that, Charlie wheeled his charge out into the main corridor and rumbled skilfully away, dodging the dinner trolleys and visitors with amazing speed.

Taking a deep breath, I turned to go down the stairs which led into the Oral Surgery Department. It seemed quiet and peaceful as I walked along, passing the outpatients' area, where the dentists' chairs were empty and the drills were still. Passing the operating theatre on the right, I peeped into the round portholes to see if there was any activity, but it too was empty.

A little further along, on the left-hand side, was the staff room. I walked in, trying not to look too nervous. Janice was sitting at the desk, just completing the Kardex in readiness for the handover. She looked up. "Oh, hello, Hilary. How are you doing?"

I could have kissed her. It was so rare to be addressed by your first name and it made all the difference in the world. "I'm terrified," I squeaked.

"Och, you'll be all right. It's really quiet today. The Prof is on holiday this week and so the operating lists are much smaller than usual. We're only expecting a couple of admissions this afternoon, one for extraction of wisdom teeth and the other for a maxillary fracture. Easy-peasy – it's a good day to start."

I locked my handbag away and sat down with my pen and notebook at the ready.

"Anyway," Janice went on, "Margery has agreed to work with you until five o'clock."

For some reason, I had completely forgotten about Margery. The mention of her name made my struggling spirits take a turn for the worse. I was technically supposed to be senior to her, as I was the full-timer. The thought of trying to ask her to do anything seemed like an impossibility. I knew that her opinion of me was very low, as I had always been quiet and willing to do as I was told as a student. How would we cope now?

I didn't have time to answer the question, as at that moment, Margery Frobisher entered in all her glory.

"That canteen just doesn't get any better," she complained. "I asked for some Earl Grey tea and did they have any? When is this place going to become civilised?"

She put her handbag away and then looked at me. "Well, now, so this is the big day, is it, Nurse McIntosh?"

"It's Staff Nurse McIntosh now, Margery," said Janice. "Doesn't she look smart in her uniform?"

"What on earth have you done to your hair?"

I couldn't believe how vulnerable I was feeling and was about to try to explain what had happened, when Janice spoke in my defence again. "I think it looks very nice. It suits you short."

I looked down at the notepad in my lap. It was blank, like my mind. If only there was a way that I could stop Margery from being so unkind all the time. I hated myself for not being tougher, and more able to give a good answer which would mean that she would treat me with some respect.

"Let's begin, then," said Janice and she went through the Report carefully and thoroughly. At the end she took me around the ward to familiarise me with the equipment and stocks of implements.

I felt shy as I walked down the ward. This was it, the moment when I faced the public as the person responsible for the care given during my shift. "I can do all things through Christ who strengthens me."

Janice went off for her lunch and Margery sat filing her nails in the nurses' room. I walked down the ward, introduced myself to all of the patients, checking that all of their observations were up to date and satisfactory, and ensuring that every patient had been written up for adequate analgesia and that they were comfortable.

Mr McTaggart, one of the patients who had been admitted for surgery to a fractured cheekbone and who was recovering well, seemed very chirpy. "Are you new, Nurse?"

"Well, I have worked here before as a student, but, yes, this is my first day as a staff nurse."

He raised his eyebrows. "Phew! Big day, eh?"

"You could say that," I smiled, hopefully confidently. "If there is anything you need, please don't hesitate to ask."

He winked at the man in the next bed. "I think we're on to a winner here, Jock", and with that, the pair of them laughed. I felt myself blush. "Oh God, when will I get to grips with all this?"

A few minutes later, our first admission for the afternoon arrived. Margery remained in the nurses' room, so I welcomed Mr Robertson and showed him to his bed. I went off in search of all the required forms and charts which were needed to complete the admission. I had real difficulty finding them all and had to ask Margery where the fluid balance charts were kept. She looked up smugly from her nails. "You keep looking, Nurse. That way, you'll not forget where they are in future, will you?"

I eventually found them under another name in the filing cabinet, but had wasted at least five minutes unnecessarily. I took a clean thermometer and the portable sphygmomanometer over to Mr Robertson's bed. "I'm sorry to have taken so long, but this is my first day today."

Mr Robertson looked anxiously at his wife. "But you do know what you are doing, don't you?" he asked me.

"Oh yes, of course," I lied.

I checked his temperature, blood pressure and pulse rate; they were all normal. I charted the results and checked his urine, which was also normal. I checked his date of birth once again and attached a name tag to his left wrist. I took him and his wife on a tour of the ward, showed them the day room, toilets and bathroom, and explained the routine of the ward. Finally, I introduced him to his neighbouring patients on either side.

Having completed this, I returned to the nurses' room to complete the admission Kardex, which described the reason for admission and the care and advice which had been given.

Halfway through this, the second admission arrived. Margery could see that I was still busy with the first, but instead of admitting the patient herself, she stood up and, smiling sweetly, simply said, "Nurse will be with you in a moment. Please take a seat."

I should have challenged her there and then, but I didn't. Consequently, I rushed the first Kardex and then had to rush around gathering all the forms and charts for the second admission. I should have been organised enough to have prepared two sets at once, but I was inexperienced and very nervous and I could feel her claws digging ever deeper.

Janice returned from lunch. "Why is that patient sitting over there?" she asked.

Margery spoke up swiftly. "Nurse McIntosh has taken so long over the first admission and has left them sitting there for ages."

I looked up pleadingly at Janice. "I'm sorry, Janice, but I had some difficulty finding all the forms. I've almost finished the first one."

"That's OK. I'll do it myself," she said. She looked at Margery as she left the room, but Margery just sat smiling to herself and checking that her claws were sufficiently sharp.

Janice finished her admission and soon it was time for me to take my afternoon break. We were situated at the furthest point from the canteen and I walked quickly along the corridor in search of a much-needed cup of coffee. The canteen was busy and I had to wait a long time to be served. I found a seat at a table with some of my group and we all shared notes on our first day in whites.

They all looked very calm and confident and I felt ashamed of myself for feeling so demoralised. Never mind. Best foot forward. It wouldn't always be this bad. With these thoughts in mind, I walked quickly back to the department.

Margery had stirred her stumps and was actually giving some analgesia to a patient who had had his wisdom teeth extracted that morning. She glared at me as I returned to the ward. "I thought that you had checked that all the patients had had their analgesia."

"I did."

"Well, why didn't Mr Tobin receive his then?"

"He said that he was comfortable."

"He says that he's been in pain for ages. Really, Nurse, you are going to have to do better than this."

Margery turned on her heel and, smiling angelically at the man in the bed, said, "I'm so very sorry. She's new, you see. That's why she made the mistake."

Mr Tobin, to his credit, looked suitably bemused. "I've only just started to feel any pain."

"There you are," Margery crooned, thrusting his cup of water in his mouth to ensure that he couldn't say any more in my defence. I smiled gratefully at him and went to put my bag away. I could tell that this was going to be less than a fun evening.

Janice left the ward at half past three and Margery and I were left to sort things out on our own. She was due to leave at five o'clock and a student nurse from Ward 31 was due to come and work with me for the rest of the shift.

At four o'clock, I set about checking all the observations of the patients.

"Which side of the ward would you like to attend to?" I asked Margery.

"I think that you should do them all, Nurse. Perhaps that way you will get quicker at it."

I couldn't believe her attitude, but, not wanting to cause a scene, I hurried around the ward, attending to the patients on my own.

Halfway around, one of the patients smiled sympathetically. "Is she giving you a hard time, Nurse?" I felt the tears prick the back of my eyes.

"Oh, it's OK. It's just that I've got a lot to learn, that's all."

Mr Bradberry took my hand. "Don't let her get you down. You're going to be a great nurse." I swallowed hard and felt my lower lip dance a silent jig as I tried to regain composure.

"Thank you. I'll just check your blood pressure again."

I think that Mr Bradberry could see that I was finding it difficult to see the readings on the sphygmomanometer through the mist of tears which was gathering. Eventually I succeeded, and carried on to the next patient.

By five o'clock my morale had plummeted through the floor and was threatening to take its holiday in Australia if the situation didn't improve rapidly. Thankfully it did, as Margery left the ward. I wondered what on earth I had let myself in for, working in this department again. I asked myself for the thousandth time why some people had to go out of their way to be so vindictive. I kept battling with the thought of retaliation, but I had always been taught that it was important to forgive others and to always treat them as you would like to be treated yourself.

My third-year student arrived on the ward shortly after five and I took her on a brief tour and introduced her to the patients. Sharon seemed very competent and was willing to do whatever was asked of her, which made a considerable and very welcome change from the previous four hours of the shift. I still found it difficult to delegate the work, but the evening passed smoothly enough and all was ready for the night staff when they came on the ward at nine o'clock.

The handover completed, Sharon and I left the ward. For a quiet shift, I felt absolutely exhausted. The threat of so much responsibility should anything go wrong, together with the constant jibes of one Margery Frobisher, were going to take some getting used to.

Chapter Twenty-Two

I didn't sleep well that night. It was partly due to the adrenalin which was still creating havoc, but also due to a small furry animal who had decided that acrobatics in the dead of night were a great idea.

Shahida hadn't mentioned that hamsters are nocturnal and I hadn't appreciated quite how busy they can be in the wee small hours. By two o'clock in the morning, lying with my head under the pillow and trying to count sheep, I decided that I was fighting a losing battle. I got up, put on the light, and took Ruby's cage out of the wardrobe.

I think she was pleased to see me. She stood up on her hind legs in the cage and looked intently into my eyes. I wondered if she could tell that I wasn't Shahida. Now, I'm not very good with small furry animals. When I was about six years old, my mum had bought us a mouse called Henrietta. The poor little thing had terrified me, and the fact that she was constantly trying to claw her way out of her cage had left me emotionally scarred where little rodents were concerned. We had to take her back to the pet shop after a few weeks.

Fifteen years on, I decided that I really should take this fear by the throat and grasp the nettle, if you see what I mean. Taking a deep breath, I removed the lid from the lower section of the cage and placed my hand inside, in an attempt to pick Ruby up. I picked up her furry, fidgeting body and gently stroked her head.

I couldn't have had a firm enough grasp because next second there was a honey-coloured fur ball running around my room at an amazing rate of knots. Although hamsters are small, they can be amazingly fast and, of course, Ruby, being a clever hamster, knew how to get the better of a mere human. Perhaps it was the fact that our diurnal rhythms were completely different, her body clock telling her that this was the time of day to go hiding under the bed, and mine telling me that I should be fast asleep on top of it.

It took me a full half-hour to finally corner her and return her to her cage. During that time, I had repeatedly moved the bed around the room and had several times become wedged underneath it. The poor nurse sleeping in the room below must have wondered what on earth was going on in the room above.

I replaced the lid on the cage with a sigh of relief and hoped that the running up and down would mean that Ruby would now be quieter for the remainder of the night. I shut the wardrobe doors and fell back into bed. I was completely shattered, but now my mind was full of thoughts of honey-coloured fur balls as well as bejewelled nurses with immaculate nails. Somehow the two images converged and in my dreams I was being chased by a giant hamster wearing diamond earrings who kept telling me that I would never be good enough.

When the alarm clock sprang into action at six o'clock, I awoke to find all of the blankets strewn over the floor. I was busily wrestling with the remaining sheet, which had been putting up a good fight. So much for a restful night.

I knelt by the bed to pray. I really needed God's help now, more than ever. As frightened as I was of making a mistake which could possibly endanger someone's life, I was just as fearful of the constant, undermining comments and unsupportive behaviour of Margery Frobisher.

"Lord, please go before me today. Please help me to care for all the people on the ward and to make sound decisions. Please, please help me with Margery, because I don't know what to do with her. Why does she have to be so unkind?"

I listened quietly for a few moments, but no answer came to that question. As I picked up my Bible reading for that day, however, I saw that it was from the Psalms – Psalm 59 in particular, which read: "I have done no wrong, yet they are ready to attack me" and "O my Strength, I watch for You; You, O God, are my fortress, my loving God. God will go before me and will let me gloat over those who slander me" (Psalm 59:4,9).

Now, I didn't want to gloat over anyone, but it would be nice not to be treated like a piece of dirt. I felt that the Lord had heard my prayer and, although I was still very tired and worried, I also had a sense that he was with me.

As I walked on to the ward, the night staff were finishing off the admission of a young man who had been involved in a road traffic accident. He had undergone maxillary surgery during the night and had his jaws wired together to support the facial fractures which he had sustained. As I sat down to take report, I was aware that I was in a sad minority of one, with one auxiliary nurse who was involved in serving breakfast at that time. I checked the duty rota and, sure enough, Margery should have been on with me. I wondered where she was. It was going to be rather tricky specialling the new admission and preparing the cases for theatre all by myself.

There was no point waiting for her; the night staff had done their bit and it was time for them to go home, so I took report on my own. As they left, I was just about to call Miss Foster, the nursing officer, to make her aware of my staff situation, when Margery appeared at the end of the ward and walked nonchalantly, and very slowly, into the staff room.

No apology, just, "Well, you'd better prep the theatre cases, hadn't you? You can remember how to do THAT, can't you?"

"Yes, I can, thank you. I think that you should know that we also have a new admission on the ward in the side room.

Russell had surgery during the night and needs to be specialled today. Would you like to look after him, or shall I?"

"I'll look after him; you can do the rest."

With that, she turned on the charm and walked into Russell's room with a huge smile on her face, greeting the poor man with a voice dripping with false concern. The incoherent grunt which came from the bed at least gave me a little hope that Margery's day might be a little less easy than she might have imagined.

Back in the main ward, I was busily preparing the two theatre cases. Each patient had two name tags and was dressed in a theatre gown. All jewellery was removed, together with dentures, and all valuables were itemised and sealed in brown envelopes and locked away. The pre-meds were administered, which were supposed to help the patients relax prior to surgery, but in Mr Robertson's case, they seemed to be having the opposite effect.

Mr Robertson was pacing up and down the ward, seemingly unworried by the gaping gown which left his posterior in full view of the other patients.

"I really don't want an operation, you know," he kept saying. "I'm sure that it's not entirely necessary, all this. In fact, I think that I'll just get dressed and go away home."

He made a lunge for the bedside locker in an effort to retrieve his clothes.

"Now, Mr Robertson," I said, "there's nothing to worry about. What I need you to do is lie down on your bed, and try and relax. The operation will not take very long and it will heal very quickly once the bones have been reunited in the correct position. If you don't have the surgery, you could be left with a facial deformity, and the bones could also be prone to infection."

He thought about this for a moment and then swung his feet back on to the bed. "Well, if you're sure, Nurse."

At that very moment, one of the consultants arrived on the ward and asked to do a round. I grabbed the trolley containing the patients' notes and prayed that they would be in order and up to date. I was very nervous as the round progressed, as I had never been responsible for a ward during a morning shift before.

The consultant seemed pleased with his patients' progress and he reassured Mr Robertson that all would be well. As he left the ward for the theatre he turned to me and said, "You're new here, aren't you?"

"Yes, Mr Johnstone. This is my second day here."

"Well, keep up the good work."

With that, he disappeared into the theatre with his entourage of doctors and students who would be assisting and observing him in action in a very few minutes' time. I was attempting to assist the other patients in their post-operative oral hygiene regimes, as well as their general washes and toileting, according to their needs, when the porter turned up with a theatre trolley to take Mr Robertson to theatre. At that same moment, Margery appeared out of the side room asking for the keys to the drugs cupboard in order to give Russell some more analgesia. I said that I would be able to check the medication with her just as soon as Mr Robertson was safely transported to theatre.

That, however, was not good enough for Margery. "My patient is in pain and you are saying that he has to wait until you are ready before he can obtain any relief? What kind of nurse are you?"

My heart thudded in indignation. She knew very well that I was trying to do the job of at least two people out here on the ward, whilst she sat and read a magazine, watching over a man as he slept post-operatively.

"I will be with you in a minute," I said.

"Give me the keys now and I will draw up the medication," Margery demanded. This left me in a quandary. All controlled drugs should be drawn up in the presence of two members of nursing staff; otherwise, they should not be administered at all. This was to minimise the risk of any errors in dosage, or, God forbid, any of the drugs going missing.

"Give me the keys!" barked Margery. In my inexperience, I handed the keys over to her and escorted the still-chattering Mr Robertson to his fate in theatre. I walked briskly back to the ward and expected to find Margery next to the drugs cupboard, waiting to draw up the medication. She was nowhere to be found. I rushed into Russell's room to find her injecting the omnopon into his thigh. The expression on my face must have said it all.

"Don't worry," said Margery, "I got the auxiliary to check it with me."

In that one sentence, Margery had managed to convey just exactly what she thought. In her eyes, I was no better than an unqualified helper and she was going to take every opportunity that she could to prove it.

"May I have the keys, please?" My voice came out huskily.

"Why do you want them?" she asked.

"I need to check the drugs and the drugs book. I presume that the auxiliary didn't sign the book as well?"

Margery grudgingly handed the keys back to me and I hurriedly checked that the stock in the cupboard, and the record in the book, were the same. I had checked the ampoule in Russell's room, to ensure that the correct drug and dosage had been administered. Thankfully, the records tallied. I heaved a sigh of relief.

Margery knew that if there had been any discrepancies then I would have been the one to blame, as the staff nurse in charge of the ward at the time. I tried to clear my mind of the situation, and carried on with caring for the remaining fifteen patients on the ward.

I had just about got on top of all the necessary tasks when Mr Robertson was brought back from theatre. He was still very drowsy but was managing to shout and wave his arms around alarmingly.

"He's been like this ever since the anaesthetist took the ET tube out, apparently," said the porter. "Bit of a nutter if you ask me."

I wasn't asking him and all I really needed was his help to lift Mr Robertson on to his bed and to take Mr Donnolly, who had been waiting patiently for his turn in theatre. The problem was that Mr Robertson was waving his arms so wildly that I was frightened that he might just propel himself out of bed.

"Could you get me some cot sides, please?" I asked the porter. He scowled and said, "It's not my job to do that."

"Well, unless you do, I cannot leave this patient and allow you to take the next to theatre, so it's up to you."

He thought about it for a moment. "OK, seeing as you asked so nicely." I shuddered as he leered and trundled off in search of the cot sides which would prevent Mr Robertson from rolling out of bed.

Five minutes can seem a long time when you are trying to talk sensibly to a person who is completely high following an anaesthetic. I tried to gently restrain the flailing arms and managed to catch a fist in my face for my troubles. Mr Flintoff in the opposite bed spoke up, as my eyes were streaming as a result of the impact on my nose. "Are you all right, Nurse? That was a good left hook he caught you with there."

I tried to smile reassuringly at Mr Flintoff, "I'm fine, thank you. It's all part of the job." By then, my nose and my eyes were streaming, but I couldn't reach the handkerchief in my pocket without letting go of at least one of Mr Robertson's hands. I decided that that was too much of a risk, so I hung on grimly and prayed that the reluctant porter would come back soon.

Standing there with my eyes and nose running, I noticed the side room door open and Margery Frobisher stuck her immaculate head around the door.

"Is everything all right?" she cooed. I could tell that she was thoroughly enjoying the spectacle.

"I'm just waiting for the porter to bring some cot sides."

"Oh, is that what you were doing? I thought that you might be molesting the patient. It certainly looks that way from here."

At that moment, the porter returned, bearing two cot sides. I could have hugged him. Together, we attached the sides to the bed and secured them so that Mr Robertson would be safe. Ironically, he was beginning to calm down now and was snoring peacefully by the time that we had finished.

The porter and I then went to Mr Donnolly's bed. He was looking pale and worried.

"You don't think that the anaesthetic will make me like that, do you?" he asked anxiously, as we drew the curtains around the bed.

"Oh, no, Mr Donnolly," I said. "Most people have a really good sleep following the anaesthetic. I am sure that you will be fine."

He seemed happier and managed to lift himself on to the trolley with very little help from either of us. I checked that the notes were correct and that they included the latest observation chart, and escorted Mr Donnolly down the corridor to theatre.

By now, it was 10:30 a.m. and Margery appeared once again, stating that it was time for her coffee break. She walked past me and, taking her handbag, marched out of the ward and off to the canteen. This left me alone with one auxiliary, a patient who needed to be specialled, fourteen other patients on the ward, and another due to return from theatre very shortly.

The antics of the preceding night were beginning to take their toll and I could feel the waves of fatigue beginning to crash into my brain. What should I do next? Before I could answer that one, the phone rang. It was Casualty. They had an admission for us, another maxillary fracture following an assault. The Casualty doctor warned me that the patient was aggressive and still under the influence of a large intake of alcohol. Great.

I quickly prepared a bed and charts in readiness for the new admission and was just checking Mr Robertson's post-operative observations when the trolley bearing my latest charge came trundling down the corridor.

I'm not sure to this day whether I heard the trolley first or whether it was the shouting of obscenities which was first to reach my ears. Whichever it was, the next moment Gavin Henries appeared in full technicolour glory and larger than life.

I think it is safe to say that there have been few individuals who have made such an impression upon virtually all of my senses simultaneously. The man was huge – the trolley could barely contain him. His clothes were matted with a combination of dirt, sweat, blood, alcohol and vomit, and the odour was overwhelming. He was swearing loudly and continuously: "Get your dirty hands off me, ya filthy mare!" I knew that I had my hands full.

The porters and I exchanged looks of "Rather you than me" and, "How are we going to get this man on to the bed and get any sense of cooperation from him?"

I decided that assertiveness was the best policy in a situation such as this. "Come on, Gavin, it's time you stopped shouting at everyone and helped us to help you." I said this in a voice which I hoped would sound brave and confident, but underneath I was shaking in my lily-white shoes.

Gavin looked at me as straight as a man can who has swallowed two bottles of whisky.

"Are y' telling me what to do, ya wee whippersnapper? What right have ye to tell me t' do anything at all? If I dinnae want tae move, I'm bloomin' well no' gonnae!" He folded his arms defiantly across the huge expanse which was his chest.

"That's all very well, Gavin, but we cannot help you if you are not willing to work with us."

The porters were beginning to get fidgety and were looking at their watches. It was time for their coffee break and they needed to return the trolley to Casualty.

I tried a change of tack. "Would you like me to run you a bath, so that you can get out of those dirty clothes and get changed into some of our clean ones?" I could see the words wobbling unsteadily across his brain as his facial expression changed from one of absolute defiance to one of uncertainty.

"Och, well maybe I will stay then, hen. That's exceedingly generous of you."

Oh, no, I thought. He was now going through the soporific stage which too much alcohol seems to induce. There was no way that he could be safely left in a bathroom without supervision. I felt a twinge of guilt as he willingly rolled himself on to the bed in readiness for the ablutions which would, in reality, have to wait a while to take place. The bed groaned and creaked as Gavin landed and the trolley and porters almost vanished into thin air as soon as the transition had been made.

I was beginning to feel very vulnerable as the porters left. In my care was Russell, who had not been observed for at least 20 minutes, Mr Robertson, who was still singing and waving to all and sundry, and now Gavin, adding his own bouquet to the assembled patients, who were sitting in or on their beds with rather anxious expressions on their faces.

Where was Margery?

Chapter Twenty-Three

Twenty minutes later, Margery Frobisher arrived back on the ward. The coffee break was meant to be fifteen minutes maximum and, by my calculations, she had been away for at least 45.

"Everything all right?" she smirked as she sauntered past me. Before putting her handbag away, she sprayed herself liberally with an expensive perfume. "Have you done Russell's obs for me?"

"I haven't had time. Since you have been away, I have had to deal with Mr Robertson, who was in danger of injuring himself post-operatively, I have taken Mr Donnolly to theatre, and I have had to admit a man who is vilely drunk. I'm afraid that Russell's observations are not up to me today."

"Are you saying that you left him unattended whilst I have been away?"

"I did check on him and he was fine, but I have just not been able to do everything single-handed."

Margery turned on her heel. "And you call yourself a nurse?" She knew that I was inexperienced and that I did not have the confidence to tackle her about her unreasonably long break. Without any concern for anyone else, she entered Russell's room, sat down, and began reading the latest magazine.

There was a trundling sound: Mr Donnolly was returning to his bed following the extraction of his wisdom teeth. He was moaning gently and was shivering after the anaesthetic. Blood loss seemed minimal and his pulse rate was satisfactory, so I was happy to accept him back on the ward.

"Mr Donnolly, you're back on the ward now and we're just going to lift you into your bed."

The porters and I slid him across; I covered him with the sheet and blankets, and placed the emergency buzzer in his right hand, explaining that he was to use this if he needed any help at all. He nodded in agreement and then went soundly back to sleep.

I could feel my own blood sugar dropping rapidly and was very grateful when Laura, the auxiliary, tapped me on the shoulder and told me that Mrs Brown was waiting for me in the kitchen. I added three sugars to the tea and gulped it down.

Back on the ward, Gavin was moving rapidly through aggression, into depression, and was now in the agitated phase which so often follows a large intake of alcohol. I called the senior house officer, advising him that Gavin needed to be seen and assessed as soon as possible.

"I'm just having my coffee," he said. "I'll be there in a few." Lucky him, I thought. I bet that was a doughnut he was eating as well.

I rushed through the routine medicine round for the remaining patients on the ward and then rapidly checked all the observations. All seemed well, until I came up to Mr Donnolly, who was still sleeping.

I knew that there was something wrong as soon as I approached his bed. His pillow was suddenly crimson and he was bleeding profusely from the wounds in his mouth. Thankfully, he was lying on his side and this had prevented him from choking on the blood which was now flowing fairly freely from his traumatised gums.

I rushed to open the emergency post-operative pack beside his bed and, calling to him, explained that I needed to pack his mouth with gauze and that he needed to bite down hard on the packs in order to stop the bleeding.

Mr Donnolly woke up and spat a large quantity of blood and saliva down my white uniform. There were large clots amongst the debris; I rolled the gauze quickly and inserted two rolls either side at the back of his mouth. "You must bite down hard, Mr Donnolly, as this will help to stop the bleeding. You must keep biting down; do you understand?"

A muffled "Yeff" and a nod of the head indicated that he knew what he had to do. I rapidly changed his pillow and helped him out of the theatre gown and into his own pyjamas, and gave him a wash to help him to feel more comfortable. I covered my uniform with a plastic apron and was just pulling back the curtains when Dr Shawberry arrived on the ward.

"I'm so glad you're here," I said. "This is Mr Gavin Henries. He had a maxillary fracture following an assault earlier today. He has been rather the worse for wear, following a large intake of alcohol. He needs admitting and assessing, please."

"He needs rather more than that, I would say." Dr Shawberry briefly held his nose and then, taking a deep breath, he introduced himself to the now depressed giant.

"Hello there, Mr Henries. My name is Dr Shawberry. I'm just going to examine you to make sure that you are fit enough to undergo an anaesthetic to mend the wee fracture you have in your cheekbone there."

Gavin manfully attempted to focus on the face which was talking to him. "Och, I dinnae need an operation, Doctor," he said. "Wha' I need is a drink."

"I think that you've had quite enough of that for one day, don't you?"

Gavin pulled his huge body forward in the bed and, almost nose to nose with Dr Shawberry, speaking very slowly, said, "No. No, I dinnae think I have. And I should ken. It's my body after all."

"Indeed it is your body, Mr Henries, and I would just like to help you to get better."

"Och, dinnae gie me that', ye wee tosspot. In fact, I think tha' I'm all right now and I think tha' I'll be getting away home."

With that, he swung his enormous legs out of bed and prepared to launch himself down the ward in his bid for freedom. Dr Shawberry and I looked at each other, neither of us knowing quite what to do next. There was no way that we could physically restrain him, as Gavin could have knocked us aside with his little finger if he so chose. As it was, we were saved by him tottering slowly from side to side; on the third lunge, I grabbed both of his legs and swung him quickly back into bed.

Gavin looked up at the ceiling and moaned gently. "Why the heck don't ye have a ceiling tha' stays still?" I looked up at the ceiling, but it seemed perfectly still to me. I looked back at Gavin, whose eyes seemed almost to be revolving independently of one another in their sockets.

"I think that I'll come back and assess him in an hour. He'll probably be more compos mentis then." Dr Shawberry got up to leave the ward, but I reminded him that Mr Donnolly had had a heavy post-operative bleed and that he needed an assessment because of this.

Mr Donnolly was still dutifully biting down on the gauze when Dr Shawberry went to see him. "Nurse tells me that you have had a bit of a bleed, Mr Donnolly?"

"Yeff, Doctor."

"I'll just take a wee look at the gums to see if the bleeding has stopped. Open wide." Dr Shawberry removed the sodden gauze swabs and, using my pen torch, had a look at the wound sites.

"They seem OK now," he said to me. "Let me know if there is any more bleeding, because he may need a couple of sutures in there if this doesn't stop."

Mr Donnolly looked worried and I tried to reassure him. "Settle down and try to have some rest." With that, he lay down and closed his eyes.

It was lunchtime and the trolley came rolling into the ward. Most of the patients were on a soft diet and I rushed around the ward with Laura, serving the food to the lucky few who were able to eat. My stomach was grumbling loudly. The silent protest was over – it wanted food and it wanted it NOW!

On cue, Margery's immaculate hairdo appeared around the door frame of the side room. "It's time I went for my lunch. I'm off now. Russell's still sleeping and there haven't been any problems. 'Bye." With that, she swung her handbag over her shoulder and sauntered slowly out of the ward.

Laura looked heavenwards and I bit my tongue. "Who does she think she is?" said Laura. "You should be the one having a break, not her. She's spent the morning sitting reading a magazine and you've been running up and down non-stop."

The unexpected sympathy had its usual effect: the injustice of the situation caused mixed emotions of anger and sadness, and a feeling of powerlessness left me with a huge lump in the back of my throat. I said nothing. I continued clearing away the lunch trays, then went into the office to write up all of the nursing notes in readiness for the late staff who were due to arrive in about 20 minutes' time.

I wrote quickly and had almost finished when Janice arrived. "Hiya!" she said brightly. "How's your first early-in-charge gone?"

I didn't feel able to speak, so I just shook my head and carried on writing.

Sister Dewhurst arrived a moment later and I felt so ill-prepared. I gave report and then went into Russell's room to check on his half-hourly observations. Whilst I was in there, I heard Margery's voice in the nurses' room, which was adjacent to the side room. She was talking to Sister Dewhurst.

"You should have seen her, Sister; she was running around the ward, not getting anything done. She left me to check the omnopon on my own and failed to check on Russell whilst I was on my coffee break. She is just incompetent."

Something happened in that moment. All of my upbringing had made me shy away from confrontation, and all of my Christian teaching had taught me to turn the other cheek and not to deride others. But she had gone too far. I completed Russell's obs and walked quickly into the nurses' room. I closed the door quietly and looked Margery straight in the eye.

"That's it," I said. "I have had just about enough of your behaviour, Margery. You have been so critical and unsupportive. I have been coping with the whole ward virtually single-handed because you have refused to help me. You have abused your position by taking far too long for your breaks and not allowing me to take a break at all. In fact, you are nothing more than a bully and I'm not going to put up with it any longer."

Margery's face was a picture. The self-satisfied leer had vanished and in its place was a look of open-mouthed disbelief. The worm had turned, and sooner than she had expected. I stood silently before her, awaiting her reaction. I had seldom dared to express negative views so directly before and I was wondering what to do next.

Sister broke the silence. "I think that it would be a good idea if you went for a lunch break now, Hilary." She spoke quietly and I took the hint. Taking my handbag from the locker, I turned and walked briskly away, before anyone could see the tears of frustration which were beginning to roll down my face.

As I walked back to the nurses' home, I muttered darkly to myself, "I've run up and down the ward all morning, have been sworn at, punched on the nose, had patients bleeding all over me and threatening to haemorrhage, and have been insulted and told lies about. What on earth am I doing in a place like this?"

I rushed upstairs to my room and flung myself on the bed. I was so tired, but my head was spinning with all of the morning's events. I changed out of the uniform and into a fresh one, and then made myself a sandwich.

Ten minutes later, it was time to be heading back to the ward. I felt apprehensive, now that my blood was no longer up. What sort of trouble would I be in, now that I had spoken my mind so freely? Quietly, I walked back into the nurses' room and was putting my handbag away when Sister spoke.

"Now, Hilary, I need to have a wee word."

"Yes, Sister."

"Sit down. Now, why don't you tell me what has gone on here this morning?"

So, as accurately as possible, I recounted the morning's events. Sister listened attentively. When I had finished, she began to speak again.

"Now, I know that Margery has a strong personality and she can take a little getting used to, but she assures me that she will try to give you as much support as possible in future."

"Thank you, Sister," I tried to sound positive, but inwardly was feeling very doubtful.

"Right, well I think that you should get home at least half an hour early today, as you have missed breaks and have been so short of staff."

"Thank you, Sister."

"That will be all."

"Yes, Sister." I stood up and walked back on to the ward in readiness to check the two o'clock observations. Janice was administering the medications. She looked up from the drugs trolley and smiled reassuringly. "Are you all right?"

"Yes, thank you."

"Don't let her get you down," she whispered. "She gave me hell when I first started and, from what I've heard, you did a good job of putting her back in her place."

In spite of myself, I could feel my spirits beginning to rise. Margery had gone home and, for a little while at least, I could get on with my job without the daggers being drawn. Tomorrow would be another day.

Chapter Twenty-Four

The days did pass and things did improve. Margery and I kept our distance and I noticed with relief that she seemed to be getting on with her job. Janice remained my preferred choice of working partner as she was always calm and supportive, and seemed to bring an aura of peace wherever she went.

Months went by, but in spite of the improvement, I still had a nagging feeling that this was not the place for me. I started making enquiries amongst my other colleagues about possible posts in other areas of the hospital.

By this time, Shahida had forgiven me for not handling Ruby since our midnight escapade. She had finished her pre-registration and was now working as a staff nurse in the Accident and Emergency Department, and she was loving it. The variety and the challenge of it all meant that she was in her element. Shahida seemed to thrive on the difficult situations she encountered there and, although it made her very tired, she felt happy and fulfilled.

"I don't believe how many drunks I had to deal with today, Hilary," she said one day, as she came off an early shift and was pulling off her shoes. "Ooh, sorry, my feet smell."

"That's OK; do you want to use some deodorant?"

"Thanks. Oh, that's much better. My poor feet have run miles today."

I made her a cup of tea and we chomped our way through the remainder of a packet of biscuits whilst we talked about our respective days. I felt guilty that I was not saving the world in the same way and that my job was in a little back-water of the vast hospital complex, whereas Shahida's was at the very cutting edge.

"What's up, Hil?"

"I just feel a bit despondent. Here you are, saving lives and doing a job that really makes a difference, and all I do is trot around a little ward, admitting and discharging patients, and dealing with the odd emergency."

"Your job is just as important, Hil. People still need your gentleness and care, and you are learning much more about administration than I am and that's really important for when you want to move on."

"I wouldn't mind moving on sooner rather than later, if I'm honest, but I just don't know where to look."

"I'm sure that the right door will open at just the right time."

Several weeks went by. I was doing my best to be positive, but was failing miserably. The monthly Hospital Christian Fellowship tea was coming up and, as usual, was being held in Laura Somerville's rooms.

I took along a packet of tea and some cakes, and joined the others for a high tea which always served to raise the spirits of even the most stoically demoralised.

I took the cakes into the kitchen.

"Hilary, I'm glad you're here!" Laura took me by surprise.

"Oh?"

"Yes. I've got a proposition for you."

"What is it?" I had an awful feeling that it was going to be something bad. Perhaps she was going to tell me that I needed to stop looking so glum and pull myself together. The fact that I was already pulling pretty hard didn't seem to matter.

"Come and sit down over here."

Oh, Lord, I thought. What am I going to do if they sack me? The thoughts came racing through my mind as I sat down dumbly.

"Don't look so worried, Hilary," Laura said. "I would like to offer you a job."

I continued to sit dumbly, but with my mouth opening and closing silently, like a huge fish.

"Well, what do you think?"

What could I think? Not only was Laura the nursing officer for the Coronary Care Unit, but it was also the largest unit of its kind in the whole region. It would offer me the challenge and experience that I was craving. It was an unbelievable honour to be offered such a position. I was truly amazed. My voice squeaked as I tried to reply.

"I can't believe it. Do you really mean it? I would love to work in CCU!"

"Well, that's settled then. You can start at the beginning of the month. I'll let Miss Foster, your present nursing officer, know of the situation. There shouldn't be any problems."

"Won't it matter that I don't have an extra qualification in intensive care nursing?" I was suddenly starting to panic as the reality of the situation and the associated responsibilities were beginning to hit home.

"That won't matter. You will be a junior member of staff and will not be expected to take charge of the unit until you have had a great deal of experience. You could be seconded to undertake further training at a later date if you so chose."

"Why have you chosen me for this? I really don't think that I deserve this opportunity."

"You really must believe in yourself, Hilary. You are an excellent nurse. I wouldn't have asked you if I didn't believe you could do the job and do it well. CCU is full of highly qualified nurses who are excellent technicians. What it lacks is someone with real warmth and compassion which will make such a difference to those patients and their families."

I sat in the kitchen for a few moments. What had Shahida said? "The right door will open at the right time."

"Thank you. Thank you so much for believing in me. I will do my best."

"I know you will, Hilary. Now, come and have some tea. It's getting cold."

I stood up and followed Laura through into her lounge. I sat down next to Shahida.

"What have you two been up to in there?" she asked me.

"I'll tell you later," I said. I couldn't share the news with anyone just yet. My world, and my career, had just taken a U-turn and I needed a little while before letting anyone in on the secret.

Miss Foster was less than impressed with the latest news and scolded me for not having informed her that I was looking for another position. I apologised profusely and tried to explain that the post in CCU had been so unexpected.

I explained the situation to Sister Dewhurst, Janice, and finally to Margery, who simply said, "Do you think that you will cope there?"

I smiled at her and said, "Miss Somerville seems to think so, so I hope that she is right."

The remaining three weeks in Oral Surgery seemed to drag and I found it difficult to remain focussed. I raided the local medical library and started reading up everything I could on the heart and reading ECGs. There was so much to learn and I felt inadequate for the task ahead. I had been introduced to some of the staff there and was overawed by their knowledge and composure, and by their skill in using all of the equipment which was present in the unit.

The night before my first shift, I was in church. The sermon was based upon Jeremiah 29:11: "I know the plans I have for you . . . plans to prosper you and not to harm you, plans to give you hope and a future." Once again I found myself hanging on to the promises of God with all of my heart and strength. It was the only way that I was going to deal with the demands of my new job.

When the morning did finally arrive, I was dressed and ready by half past six, a full hour before I was due on duty. I kept telling myself that nobody would expect me to know everything on my first day, but the doubts about my abilities kept crowding my mind. I felt sick with worry by the time I walked through the large wooden doors.

"Hullo, Hilary!" It was Sister Barnham. She was a pocket dynamo with tremendous energy and enthusiasm for her work. She gave the impression that nothing on earth would make her panic and that she was entirely bomb-proof. A good person to be working with – I could panic enough for both of us.

We took report whilst watching the twelve ECG screens from the nurses' station. Normal sinus rhythm, normal sinus rhythm, partial heart block, sinus tachycardia, slight bradycardia . . . the patterns danced and cavorted in front of our eyes. As I listened to report, I tried to relate the conditions described to the people who lay in the single rooms. Some looked so pale, and others were sitting reading the morning paper. One patient was smiling and waving to us all – I hoped that he would be my charge, but was informed that he was about to be transferred back on to the general area on the adjacent Ward 31.

"Right, Hilary . . ." Sister Barnham was busily checking the defibrillator paddles which were used to shock a patient's heart during a cardiac arrest when the heart was fibrillating, or fluttering ineffectively. "I'll give you a tour of the unit so that you will be able to find things."

The tour was fast and furious and curtailed by the arrival of the porters who were ready to transfer Mr Bellings back to the ward.

"Perhaps you could do the transfer, Hilary, and we'll make up the bed in readiness for the next patient."

"Yes, Sister."

I walked into Mr Bellings' room and gathered up all his belongings. I suddenly remembered that I would need to remove the ECG leads from his chest before he could leave the unit, so I did this, not realising that I should have switched the machine off prior to his. Consequently, the air was filled with the sound of the alarm wailing loudly at the nurses' station. Sister came rushing in to make sure that the patient was all right.

"Remember to switch it off next time," she said.

"I'm really sorry, Mr Bellings."

"That's OK, Nurse. Are you new here?"

"Yes. How could you guess?"

"Don't worry. I'm sure you'll soon get used to it." I wished that I shared his optimism.

We made our way on to the ward and transferred all the information from Mr Bellings' admission on CCU to one of the staff nurses there. I saw that he was settled comfortably in bed and then returned to the unit.

In the short time that I had been away, CCU had received a call from Accident and Emergency to say that a new admission was imminent. The patient was an elderly woman who had been found collapsed in one of the back streets of the city. A member of the public had begun resuscitation and this had been continued throughout the journey to hospital in the ambulance.

A couple of moments later, the doors swung open and Mrs Crocket arrived with an endotracheal tube in place and an anaesthetist ventilating her via an ambubag. She already had several intravenous lines in place and was connected to an ECG machine, the tracing of which seemed to be leaping chaotically with every movement of the trolley.

I leapt out of the way of the trolley and watched in amazement as two of the nurses immediately organised all of the necessary equipment, setting up the ventilator, intravenous monitors and cardiac monitor with split-second precision. There was no doubting that this unit was a well-oiled machine.

"Go and help Dr Samuels in Room 8, Hilary. He's doing an echo scan at the moment and he might need some help."

I found Room 8 and remembered from report that this was the patient who had had a small heart attack, or MI, a couple of days previously. He was a relatively young man, aged only 44, and the medical staff had decided that they wanted to scan his heart to check for any further damage and to see if surgery could be of benefit in the form of coronary artery bypass grafts.

As I entered the room, Dr Samuels was sitting on the bed, staring at the screen and passing a probe over Mr Gillings' chest. Mr Gillings was very pale and he was beginning to breathe very heavily. Instinctively, I held his hand and tried to reassure him.

"It's OK, Mr Gillings. Everything is going to be all right."

Dr Samuels looked up from the screen and seemed annoyed that anyone should interrupt his work.

Mr Gillings began to sweat profusely and his colour was terrible.

"Give him some oxygen, Nurse."

With trembling hands, I fumbled for the mask and switched the oxygen flow on to four litres per minute. I gently passed the mask over his face. Mr Gillings' eyes were beginning to roll and he looked terrified. I thought to myself that if he should need any adrenalin, he could definitely have some of mine – I was terrified too.

"He's arrested!"

Dr Samuels stopped probing and helped me to remove the head of the bed. I supported Mr Gillings' upper body as I removed the pillows from behind him. As his head went down, his feet shot up in the air as his whole body went into spasm, a result of the lack of oxygen to his brain. A jug of water on his bedside cabinet went splashing and crashing to the floor and I was ankle-deep in sodden pillows, wrestling with an unconscious man whose body was doing its own thing.

"God God, Nurse! What the hell do you think you are doing?"

It was a fair question, but at that moment I was not in much of a position to give a measured reply. Sister Barnham came bursting into the room. "Set up the IV sodium bicarbonate, Hilary."

I prised my hand free from Mr Gillings' clenched fist and grabbed the bag of "soda bic" from the crash trolley. I tore open the giving set and ran the liquid through as quickly as possible, tapping a few air bubbles out of the administration set.

Dr Samuels was busy administering a pre-cordal thump to Mr Gillings' chest to see if this would help his heart's rhythm return to normal. Sister was charging the defibrillator. The door opened again and this time the room was entered by the duty anaesthetist.

"That was pretty good going," said Dr Samuels, smiling.

"Was just passing, don't you know?" Dr Smythe slipped quickly up to the head of the bed, but unfortunately had not reckoned on the oxygen tubing which was suspended above one of the pillows on the floor. Next moment, he tripped on the tubing and then skidded on the wet floor before finally arriving at his destination in the proximity of Mr Gillings' head.

"Who on earth left that there?"

All eyes in the room glared silently and angrily in my direction and I felt flushed with shame and embarrassment.

"I'm sorry," I muttered, but was interrupted by the sound of the defibrillator, which was beeping to state that it was now fully charged and ready for action.

"Stand clear! Shocking!" Dr Samuels administered a shock to Mr Gillings' chest. We all stared at the ECG monitor, hoping and praying that normal sinus rhythm would return. It didn't; the machine continued to churn out reams of paper, recording the crazy and frenetic action of a dying heart.

"Hold his head back, Nurse; I'm trying to pass a tube, but just can't see his vocal chords clearly enough." Dr Smythe was struggling to gain access to Mr Gillings' airway, so I did my best to help. "Got it!" The endotracheal tube was inserted and the cuff inflated quickly.

I attached the soda bic to Mr Gillings' infusion, but, as I did so, I managed to spill some of the infusion on the floor. My hands were shaking so much that it was a struggle to connect the two ends together.

Eventually, I managed to do so, as Dr Samuels was preparing for another attempt at defibrillation. "I think that he has a tamponade – he is bleeding into his heart muscle and this is causing his heart to be unable to beat. Get me a spinal needle."

Sister Barnham was busy drawing up some lignocaine and she nodded in the direction of the door. "They're in the main crash trolley – second drawer down."

I scuttled out of the room, relieved to be out of the high-pressure environment, but driven now by a sense of urgency because every second counted for this man's survival. The needle could possibly draw off the blood which was building up between the heart muscle and the inflexible membrane which surrounded it, and acting like a tourniquet. This was constricting the heart so that it could not fill with blood with each beat, and the heart's action was therefore ineffective. The large spinal needle could possibly remove this fluid from the pericardium, and allow the heart to beat effectively again.

I rummaged in the drawer, but couldn't find the needle. I looked around desperately for another nurse who could possibly help me. They were all very busy caring for their own patients. I dashed back to Mr Gillings' room. Ashamed, I told Sister that I had been unsuccessful.

Dr Samuels turned and glared at me. "Where on earth have you come from? Don't you know that this is an intensive care area? You should know where things are and, if you don't, what good are you to anyone?"

I felt my stomach drop to my feet. I felt utterly ashamed and demoralised. What good was I to anyone if I couldn't even fetch and carry properly? A lump came to my throat.

"Try the next drawer down," Sister suggested.

I rushed back to the trolley and eventually found the needle in question. I returned to the room triumphantly, only to find the anaesthetist removing the endotracheal tube. "He really didn't stand a chance. Time of death: 10.31."

I stared in horror at the pale body in the bed, surrounded by wet pillows, a broken plastic jug, and wires and infusions which had failed to save his life. The monitor continued to spew its sorry tale; the line which had once shown the action of a live but sick heart was now flat. Life was extinct.

I looked at Sister, who was busily removing leads and infusions. She looked calm and serene, as though this was something she saw almost every day – something she had come to know as familiar. All I could feel was guilt. If only I had been quicker finding the needle, perhaps Mr Gillings would be alive now?

I set about tidying the mess surrounding the bed. As the doctors left, talking about their proposed game of golf, I apologised to Sister Barnham once again.

"I'm so sorry. I made such a mess of that, didn't I?"

"It could have been worse, Hilary. You could have killed Dr Smythe too."

She smiled and I couldn't help feeling that perhaps that might not have been such a bad thing.

Chapter Twenty-Five

By the end of that day, I felt that I had made the biggest mistake of my life. Perhaps I had been too proud to realise my limitations and should never have accepted the post in CCU. I thought that I had started to learn how to be a good nurse, but the day's events had severely dented my frail confidence.

Following the death of my patient, I had been left in charge of the grieving relatives. This had been terrible in its own right. Despite all the previous three years' encounters with death and bereaved relatives, nothing had prepared me for the tear-stained young woman who had wept hysterically over her husband whilst her two young sons stood silently staring at the body of their father.

I didn't know what to say. I stood with my arm around her shoulders and held her gently as the sobs of horror, grief, shock and absolute aloneness shook her entire being. "It's all right, it's all right." I kept repeating the words, probably more for my own benefit than for anyone else.

After what seemed an age, the sobbing gradually subsided. She was exhausted. I reached a hand out to the younger of the two sons, who was probably only seven years old. He pulled his hand away from mine. "Daddy, wake up, Daddy." His mother was too weak to speak, so I heard my own small and inexperienced voice attempting to make sense of a situation whilst fully realising that this was an impossibility. I fought the lump in my throat as I crouched down to speak to the little boy.

"Daddy can't wake up now," I said. "Daddy was very ill and now he has gone to sleep for ever."

"Why can't he wake up?" It was the older child, about nine, who was speaking now.

"Your Daddy has died. The doctors and nurses here have tried very hard to help him to get better, but sometimes, in spite of all our efforts, we cannot stop people from dying."

"Why couldn't you help my Daddy? He's MY Daddy and I want him to wake up, NOW!" The little boy's defiance only thinly masked the dawning realisation of what had happened.

"I know you do, my love, but we did everything we could and still your Daddy was too poorly to get better."

"Mummy! Get Daddy back! This lady doesn't know how to do it. You do! Mummy! Get Daddy back!" His little voice was cracking with the raw emotion of loss. His mother turned to him and, in an heroic gesture, she put aside her own feelings and crouched beside her sons.

"Daddy loved you two so much. You were the reason he got up each day to go to work, and then at the weekends to play football with you and take you to the park. He loved you so very much."

She kissed their bowed heads and held them closely to her heart.

"Daddy will never really leave us. We'll always remember the good things we used to do together. And remember the things he taught you about being good boys at school and always doing your homework? He'll always be with us when we go to the park. And you, Callum, when you're playing football, always remember what Daddy said about keeping your eye on the ball, and not to forget the off-side rule."

Callum nodded his little head and fought the tears which trickled down his freckled face. His father would have been very proud of him and his family.

After some time, they gathered their things and left CCU. As I laid the body out, I felt such sadness. Three lives had changed for ever today as a result of this one man's passing. No man is an island. We all need one another, and what happens to one affects so many others.

Leaving the unit at the end of the shift, I wondered whether I should ever bother coming back. To say that I had felt out of my depth was a good British understatement. I seemed to have spent the entire day apologising to all my colleagues for one shortcoming or another. I remembered back to the sermon of the previous day: "I know the plans I have for you . . ." As I headed back to the nurses' home, I could only hope that this was true.

As I walked home, all I could hear were Margery Frobisher's words: "Are you sure you will be able to cope?" I began to think that she was probably right. Walking into my room, I locked the door and slumped down on the bed. I was exhausted, demoralised and bitterly disappointed. I had so wanted to be the perfect nurse – the one who always knew how to cope with every situation. The one who had the right thing to say at just the right moment and whose care really made a difference to people's lives. I wanted to show Jesus's love to people by the way that I cared for them.

Instead, I had tripped up an anaesthetist, forgotten to turn off cardiac monitors, lost spinal needles, and been utterly incompetent when it came to dealing with relatives. It had been a catalogue of errors and I wondered if I should speak to Laura Somerville and explain that I had made a mistake, that I was not suitable material for her CCU.

I was just toying with the idea of going to her room when there was a knock at my door. I wondered if it was Laura and was so relieved to see Shahida standing there.

"Hiya! How did it go?" Shahida breezed into the room and was busily untying her shoelaces. I reached for the deodorant spray out of habit and she took it with a wry smile. "You know me and my feet too well," she said.

I sat down on the bed. "Shahida, I don't think I'm cut out for CCU."

"Why on earth not?"

"I made such a mess of things today. I didn't know where anything was, I took patients off monitors without first switching them off, and I even nearly sent an anaesthetist flying through the wall!"

"Sounds like quite a fun day to me. Which anaesthetist was it?"

When I told her, she simply grinned. "It couldn't have happened to a nicer bloke."

In spite of everything, Shahida was cheering me up and, in a few minutes, we were both laughing hysterically as she recalled some of the incidents of her first few shifts in Casualty.

"And then there was the time when I was left to deal with a woman's two-year-old son. The woman was the patient. She had cut herself badly with a kitchen knife, probably because she was distracted by her son. I tried everything I could to keep him amused, but he kept running around the department and I was left chasing after him. I ended up running right into one of the consultants, causing him to drop all his notes and papers everywhere. The little boy was heading for the entrance and I was worried that he might run under an incoming ambulance, so I couldn't pick up the papers for the consultant."

"So what did you do?"

"I carried on running and apologised later. Remember what we were taught? 'Safety always, girls!'" Shahida mimicked our tutors perfectly.

Three cups of coffee and half a packet of bourbon biscuits later, we were both feeling better. Things were back in perspective again and I was resolved to return to CCU the next day.

After a better night's sleep, I strode on to the unit as the clock showed 7:25. The night staff were busily completing their notes in readiness for report.

"Och, hello. You must be new here." It was Rupert, the charge nurse on night duty.

"Yes, I'm Hilary. This is my second shift. I'm only hoping that it will be better than my first."

"It was a bit like that, was it?"

"You could say that. Is there anything you would like me to do whilst we wait for the rest of the shift to arrive?"

"You could just check that the defibrillators are working. Plug them in and then discharge them on to that wee pad over there. It will show you how much of a charge it is delivering."

I did as he instructed and was pleased to find that it worked.

Sister Barnham arrived and smiled. "I wasn't sure whether we would see you today, Hilary."

"I'm here," I said. "I'm working on the premise that things can only get better."

"Let's hope you're right," she said and with that, she sat down and started taking the report. I listened once again to the stories behind the traces which danced and cavorted before my eyes. Suddenly, one of the traces showed a run of ectopic beats, which righted themselves spontaneously. A minute later, the same thing happened, only this time there was a long run of beats – the patient's heart was in ventricular tachycardia. This meant that the two larger chambers of the heart were pumping much too fast to allow the upper chambers to fill with blood. The consequence was that the heart was pumping much too quickly to effectively circulate the blood.

Sister and one of the other staff nurses rose as one and within two seconds were wheeling the crash trolley into the room in question. The patient was unconscious and his colour was terrible. Sister tore open his pyjama top and placed two gel pads over his chest. The defibrillator was charging; when it was ready, she applied the paddles and discharged the defibrillator. The result was miraculous. Mr

Jeffries opened his eyes and, looking a little bemused, smiled at us all and said, "It's happened again, hasn't it?"

Sister was removing the pads and buttoning up his pyjama top. "It's OK, Mr Jeffries. That's why you're in here." She and the staff nurse helped him to sit up in bed again, straightened his bedclothes and left the room whilst tidying the crash trolley. This was multi-tasking on an impressive scale.

Report continued and the night shift left for their beds. Sister allocated a 19-year-old young man to me. I was amazed that someone so young should be in CCU. In fact, I had had very little experience with younger patients, except during the psychiatric phase of my training.

I followed Sister into Rob's room. I could see by the expression on his face that this was a very angry young man who was lying in the bed in front of us.

"Good morning, Rob," Sister began. "This is Hilary and she will be taking care of you today."

"Oh God, not another angel of mercy." He rolled away from us so that he could no longer see us.

I could see from the feet and legs which protruded from the bedclothes that Rob had severe oedema. This was excessive swelling caused by a weakened heart. Rob had recently suffered from a severe viral illness which had affected the myocardium, or heart muscle. The heart was so weak that it could barely sustain an adequate circulation, even with Rob on bed rest. Numerous infusions were running with drugs to help the muscles to work more efficiently, alongside diuretic drugs which helped to remove excess fluid from Rob's circulation.

"I'll leave Rob to your tender care." With that, Sister Barnham turned and walked out of the room. I was left wondering how to communicate effectively with this young man who, realising his own mortality, was angry beyond words but did not have the strength to do anything about his situation.

"How are you feeling today, Rob?" I knew at once that this was the wrong sort of question.

"How do you think I'm feeling? Hunky-dory, thank you, Nurse!" He almost spat the final words, whilst mimicking a woman's voice.

"Sorry. That was a stupid question."

"Yes, it certainly was!"

"I understand that you are very angry."

"Ohno you don't! Have you got a knackered heart? Do you know what it is like to lie here, and have to pee into a bottle? Do you know what it is like to feel so weak that you can't even sit up in bed? Do you?" His brown eyes were blazing with indignation.

"No, Rob, I don't. And I am very sorry that you are feeling so ill. I just wanted you to know that we are all here to help you, if you will let us."

"Do whatever you like." He sank his head down on the pillow. He looked completely exhausted. Sullenness was his only attack left.

"I'm just going to check your blood pressure and your temperature, if that's OK?" Rob stuck his arm out, imitating compliance, but inwardly resenting every move I made. His obs were within normal parameters.

"Would you like me to bring you a basin so that you can have a wash?"

Rob nodded reluctantly. I set about organising his wash things and found a new set of pyjamas from amongst his belongings.

I gave him a wet flannel, but he didn't have the energy to wash his own face, so I offered to help him and he grudgingly agreed. I gently washed his neck, chest and arms and, respecting his modesty, left it at that. I brought him a mouthwash so that he could freshen his breath – he didn't have the strength even to brush his own teeth. Finally, having put on the new pyjama top and trousers, I combed his hair. He looked more comfortable but very tired. I checked his cardiac monitor, which showed occasional ectopic beats but otherwise a sinus rhythm. Rob fell asleep whilst I wrote down the observations on the nursing Kardex.

A few moments later, Dr Billingsgate, one of the CCU consultants, came into the room. Rob awoke and was irritated by the constant interruptions.

"Well, Nurse, how is our patient doing today?" asked the consultant.

I explained that Rob had very little energy and that his oedema was still marked. His fluid intake still exceeded his output, in spite of the medication.

"I see. I think that we should increase the diuretics and see if this will improve things, don't you?"

I stood there nodding obediently, alongside all the other nurses and doctors who were involved in the round that morning.

"Take some bloods, Nurse. Us and Es, creatinine, and cardiac enzymes."

"Yes, Dr Billingsgate."

"OK, Rob, we'll soon have you feeling better, don't you worry." With that, the entourage left the room.

I stood there dumbly. Did Dr Billingsgate know that I had never taken blood from a patient before? Did anyone, except me, know this shortcoming? After the previous day's succession of apologies, I decided that this was going to have to be yet another one to add to the list.

I headed for the door and just as I did so, Rebecca, one of the staff nurses who was completing a course in intensive care nursing, came into the room.

"Sister suggested that you might need a wee bit of help in taking Rob's blood samples. Is that right?" I could have hugged her. "Come with me and I'll show you where all the blood bottles are kept. Have you ever taken blood before?"

"No, I haven't. The samples were always taken by the

phlebotomists visiting the wards. I didn't realise that I was supposed to know how to do this."

"Don't worry. There's a whole lot of stuff to learn when you start somewhere new. Look at it this way: if you can take blood from patients in CCU, with their collapsed veins, you're going to be able to do it anywhere."

Rebecca proceeded to instruct me in the correct procedure for venipuncture. She showed me how to encourage veins to dilate near the surface and demonstrated the correct angle for inserting the needle.

"You'll be OK now."

"You mean, you want me to take Rob's bloods?"

"Of course. The best way to learn something is to do it for yourself."

I picked up the little cardboard tray containing the syringe, needle, swabs and the appropriate bottles, and walked back into Rob's room. The knot in my stomach which had accompanied my first intramuscular injection had agreed to come with me again now.

"Rob, I'm sorry, but I need one of your arms to take a blood sample, if that's all right?"

A groan came from the bed. Rob attempted to pull up his pyjama sleeve, but the effort was too much. I took the action as consent and rolled the sleeve up beyond his elbow. "I'm just going to put a tourniquet on your arm now. It will be tight for a little while . . ."

"Just get on with it!"

"OK."

I applied the tourniquet and gently stroked the inside of his elbow to encourage the appearance of his brachial vein. To my amazement, it popped up obligingly. Now all I needed to do was to stick a needle in it and take the blood. I've always winced when sticking needles in people and this time was no exception. Thankfully, Rob kept his eyes closed throughout. I drew back on the syringe and, miraculously, beautifully, the thick, dark red blood began to fill the syringe. "You're doing very well, Rob. Nearly all done." I wasn't sure if he heard the squeak which was supposed to be my reassuring voice.

When the syringe was full, I released the tourniquet and applied a cotton wool ball to the puncture site with tape. I filled the appropriate bottles and wrote all Rob's details on to each. My hands were shaking and it was difficult to complete all of the information in such tiny writing. I checked that the bleeding from the site had finished and pulled Rob's pyjama sleeve down again.

"Thank you, Rob. I'll just get these sent off to the lab." He half lifted his hand in acknowledgement and settled down for a short nap.

As I walked out of his room, Rebecca took a look at the tray. "Mission accomplished! I knew you could do it!"

"Thank you so much. I really didn't think I could."

"You should have more confidence in yourself." If only I could, I thought.

The bloods were sent off to the lab for analysis; Rob's ECG continued to remain the same. He was sleeping, but I continued with his quarter-hourly observations of blood pressure and heart rate until lunchtime.

Whilst tending Rob through the morning, I listened to the muffled sounds from the next room, where an elderly lady had been admitted. She had been found collapsed in the street and a passer-by had initiated CPR. I listened to the repetitive sound of the ventilator and the rolling of large pieces of equipment into and out of her room. The monitor assessing central venous pressure was, at that time, a large machine, similar in size to a washing machine; other pieces of equipment in the room had to be removed to allow it in.

The hushed, purposeful voices of the staff, and the intermittent bleep of one of the doctors in attendance, all painted a vivid picture of a dedicated and highly professional team at work.

Out at the main desk, one of the special alarms suddenly

sounded. This was applied to the most critically ill patient on the unit. It sent a scurrying of feet and the rolling of the crash trolley into the relevant room. I wondered what it must be like to be lying in one of these beds, listening to all these sounds, and feeling so vulnerable. It made me shudder.

Rob stirred. "Can I have a bottle?"

"Of course, Rob. I'll get one for you." I walked to the sluice and returned with a urinal for him. "Do you need some help?"

He glared at me. "No, I certainly don't!"

I handed him the urinal, but he didn't have the strength to lift up his bedclothes properly. There was nothing for it – I was just going to have to be purposeful and professional. Taking the bottle from him I placed it in the correct position. "Would you like me to help you to sit up a little more?" He nodded. Whilst the necessary took place, I held Rob's upper body. Of course, he was inhibited having someone present whilst performing what is usually a private function and my muscles were screaming by the time it was over. But we'd had success and that was the important thing.

I measured the urine and found that he was still retaining more fluid than he was excreting, so I went to find Sister to pass on this information. Sister contacted the senior house officer, who came to review Rob's progress. At the same time, the blood results were phoned through from the lab. It was bad news. Rob's condition was definitely deteriorating, in spite of the drugs and the total bed rest. As I looked through the window into his room, I could see a change in him, even since morning. He looked grey and his hands were swelling horribly. He was restless and uncomfortable, and his heart trace showed a widening gap between complexes which should have been sharp and narrow. With a feeling of despondency, I began to see that this young man might die.

I realised that I had been thinking that it was impossible for someone so young to die. It was a stupid presumption. Of course, young people can die, but I was young too and for the first time had to face the fact that youth does not mean invincibility. It was one of those moments when, suddenly, your mind has to expand itself to accommodate some new and very important facts, and readjust your thinking about life issues.

"We'll have to catheterise him." Dr Starkey broke into my thoughts. "Set up a trolley, will you?"

"Yes, of course."

I went to the treatment room and set up the appropriate trolley as quickly as possible. I knew that Rob would hate the procedure. It was bad enough for an elderly patient, let alone one who was still in his teens.

Dr Starkey and I went into Rob's room and explained what we were about to do, and why. Rob was too tired to argue, so, with as much decorum as possible, the doctor performed the procedure. Somehow, the presence of the catheter seemed to be a physical sign of the deterioration which was going on in the rest of Rob's body.

As soon as the procedure was over, I tidied Rob's bedclothes and cleared away the trolley. He was strangely quiet. It seemed as though he had almost entered another dimension. It worried me and I told Sister about my concerns.

"Rob is gravely ill, Hilary. The next 24 hours are critical. He will either pull through, or he won't."

"But he only had a virus! How can a virus cause so much destruction in a person's body?"

"In some ways, viruses are more destructive than bacterial infections; at least we have antibiotics which we can use to tackle those. With viruses, we have a limited armoury and it is up to the individual's own defences to overcome the intruder. In Rob's case, though, although he is a strapping young man, the virus has managed to so weaken his heart that his chances of survival are very slim."

Our conversation was interrupted by a ring at the exterior door. One of the relatives had come to visit. I went to the door and ushered Rob's mother into his room. I pulled up a seat for her to sit near her son. She had arrived clutching some grapes and some rugby magazines. As soon as she saw Rob, her expression changed.

"Hullo, Rob, it's Mum." She rubbed his hand gently.

Turning to me, she asked, "How is he doing today?"

I took a deep breath. I mustn't sound too gloomy and yet I must not give her false hope, either.

"Rob's condition is causing some concern at the moment, Mrs Hibbard. The doctors have increased some of the medication to try to help Rob's heart to recover, but at the moment, he is still not very well at all."

"I see. Thank you."

She turned away from me and began to talk quietly and gently to her son, who lay in his bed dozing and unresponsive to his mother's gentle touch. I was called away to take my lunch break; Rebecca kept an eye on his obs whilst I took a breather in the canteen. It was only as I left the unit and began walking normally down the corridor that I realised how much we all tended to tiptoe around and speak in hushed tones in there.

It was a relief to walk past one of the open doors and to catch a breath of warm autumnal air and see the sunshine again. It was invigorating and refreshing. This intensive atmosphere was going to take some getting used to.

Tongue salad was on the menu again and, finding a seat, I began to eat. A moment later, Shahida plonked herself down beside me.

"I don't believe some people," she said. "I've been working in a completely psycho department today. Either that, or I've flipped my lid myself."

"What's happened?"

"First thing this morning, I was told to take care of a

mother who had fallen down some stairs, or so she said. I was given the charge of her two delinquent toddlers for a couple of hours. That was bad enough, but then her husband turned up in the department with a carving knife and demanded to see his wife. We had to call security and they had a terrible job getting him to calm down and stop threatening us. In the end, the police were called and the man was handcuffed and taken to the station."

"His poor wife! Do you think that she will ever tell the truth about her 'accident'?"

"Probably not. You'd be amazed at the number of women who repeatedly come into the department with one injury after the other and with a succession of elaborate explanations."

"Doesn't it get you down, dealing with all these seemingly impossible people and situations?"

"It does sometimes, but then I remember that God never gives up on us, so we mustn't give up on others."

Good old Shahida – ever the optimist. I looked at my watch.

"Are you in a hurry, Hil?"

"No, it's just that I'm worried about my patient."

"That goes with the territory in CCU, doesn't it?"

"It's just that this time, he is only 19 years old."

"Oh, that is a bit on the worrying side. Do you think he's going to make it?"

"I'm really worried that he won't. A little while ago, he seemed to slip from defiance and anger into a state of acceptance. It worries me; I want him to keep on fighting."

"You can only do your best, Hil. You don't have the power to make people live or die."

"I know that, but he's so young. He has all his life ahead of him. And his Mum is lovely. I've had enough of seeing death get the upper hand."

"But death is part of life, isn't it? It's just a step through into a new phase, which we, here, don't fully understand."

"I suppose so. Look, I'd better get back. Thanks for listening."

"That's OK. Have a good afternoon."

"You too."

I walked briskly back to the unit and was relieved to find that nothing had changed in the 20 minutes I had been away.

"He's holding his own, Hilary," said Rebecca as she slipped off the stool at the nurses' station. "Try not to look so worried."

Rebecca went off for her lunch break and I took care of Rob's observations and also kept an eye on her patient, who was a 70-year-old lady who had suffered a heart attack the previous day. She seemed settled and comfortable, and her recordings were all within normal parameters. Only two hours to go and then I could walk away from all this tension.

Those two hours dragged, but Rob's condition did not change. His mother sat with him quietly whilst her son slept. Suddenly, she spoke. "He's so full of life, you know."

"I'm sure he is."

"He even tried out for the regional rugby team last year. He was one of the reserves."

"That's wonderful. You must be very proud of him."

"He's a great lad. No mother could ask for better." She wiped her eyes with the back of her hand. "He's all I have now, since his father died five years ago."

My heart ached for her. "I'm so very sorry. It must be very difficult for you to be here."

"It's terrible. I swore that I would never sit beside another hospital bed after Ted's illness, but here I am. I suppose it's my lot in life. I just wish that I could have been one of the lucky ones who never had to go through this sort of thing."

"Nobody would want to go through the experiences you have endured."

"It makes you wonder why some people get all the heartache, and others seem to get away scot-free. You must have seen a lot of people in difficult situations – do you ever wonder why some people suffer so much, and others seem to sail through life until they die in their beds at the age of 97?"

I felt uncomfortable. How could I make sense of the suffering of the world? It had been explained to me that the world is in a fallen state and that things are no longer the way God intended them to be. Why one person should suffer so much more than another, I could not tell, but I did know that, through suffering, some people seemed to grow in their inner being and become stronger and more beautiful inside. I did not think that God would inflict suffering on anyone. After all, he had given his only Son to take away the penalty for our transgressing nature, because he loves us so very much and wants us to be in a right relationship with himself and one another.

"I cannot tell why one person should suffer so much more than another. All we can do is pray that God will give us the strength to see our journey through."

Maureen Hibbard turned and looked at me for a moment. "You are very young, aren't you?"

"Yes."

"Well, don't ever lose that optimism. It might come in handy later on in life."

The note of bitterness did not go unnoticed, so I remained quiet and simply checked on Rob's observations once more. No change.

A few moments later, Sister appeared at the door. "Time to go home, Hilary."

I turned to Maureen again. "I have to go now. I hope to see you again tomorrow." She nodded, never taking her eyes off her son's pale face.

Walking out of the room, I felt a wave of relief come over me. I had only looked after one patient and yet I felt as exhausted as if I had taken care of an entire ward. When they said it was intensive care, the emphasis really needed to be on the word "intensive".

That evening, we were holding the Hospital Christian Fellowship meeting in the lounge on the third floor of the nurses' home. We were drinking coffee and talking about various issues affecting nurses in Mali, when Rob's name and face came vividly to my mind. I shivered and looked at my watch; it was four minutes past nine.

The next day, I came on duty to find that Rob had passed away. When I looked in the admissions and discharges register, it said that Rob Hibbard, aged 19, had passed away at 21:04. Rest in peace.

Chapter Twenty-Six

"How is it that everyone else seems to either be engaged, getting married, or at least going out with someone?"

Shahida and I sat commiserating over coffee in our new apartment. A couple of weeks earlier, we had been given the keys to a brand new flat on the hospital campus. We were sharing with Judith and we loved the freedom of our new home. We also had a magnificent view of Edinburgh Castle from our living room; when it was illuminated at night, it was like a living portrait, which we never tired of observing.

Shahida laughed. "Maybe it's because you're too sensitive and my feet are too smelly."

"You could be right – on both counts!"

"Thanks a bunch."

"Seriously, though, how does anyone meet anyone interesting without having to go on a pub crawl?"

"I wonder if there is anyone interesting on a pub crawl?"

"The alcohol probably numbs your senses so you don't mind if they're interesting or not."

We sat in silence for a few moments. "Do you really want to get married, Hil?"

"Yes, I do. I've always imagined myself getting married and having children some day. The problem is finding the right man. Don't you want to get married, then?"

"Eventually, but I keep feeling that there is something else that I need to do first. I have this odd feeling that I may need to work abroad before I meet my knight in shining armour."

At that moment, Judith came bursting into the living room. "Och, what a day!"

"Busy day on Ward 10?"

"You bettcha! We had three emergency admissions, all needing urgent surgery and specialling following their ops. I had only two junior students on with me. It was a nightmare!"

"Well done for surviving it. Do you want a coffee?"

"Thanks, Hil. Did I hear you talking about men again?"

"What do you mean, 'again'?" I carried on talking as I headed for the kitchen.

"You're always going on about them. I keep telling you that they're not worth the bother, really they're not."

"Maybe you're right."

"I know someone who might by your type, Hilary."

"Oh yes, and I bet he's got false teeth and a bald patch!"

"Well, almost. He's 37 and he's the brother of a friend of mine who works on Ward 10."

"What does he do?"

"He's a youth worker. She's always saying how lonely he is. Maybe you two should get together?"

Shahida smiled encouragingly. "It's about time someone put you out of your misery, Hil. You need something to take your mind off work in CCU. Perhaps then we would get some peace!"

"OK, then!" I surprised myself. "Can you tell me how to get in touch with him?"

"Are you serious?" Judith was laughing.

"Yes, I am. Nothing ventured, nothing gained."

"All right, I'll let my friend know and we'll arrange a meeting."

"Thanks."

"Don't mention it."

A week passed and then I received a phone call from Alan one evening. He sounded lovely and we arranged to meet up at a florist's shop on the corner of George Street. I was really nervous and spent an hour trying on various combinations of skirts and blouses until deciding upon the pink and blue skirt and pink blouse which I always seemed to wear.

"Knock him dead, Hil."

"Don't wait up, Shahida."

"Don't do anything I wouldn't do."

"OK, Mum."

Walking down the Mound, I was beginning to seriously question my sanity. I went through the emergency checklist in my mind: he had to be a Christian, no sex before marriage, no alcohol on the first date, and act as cool as possible.

I had been standing on the corner, watching the world going home after work, looking out for a man of medium height with dark hair and a moustache. There were loads of men fitting that description and I was just beginning to give up hope, when Alan came bounding up.

"Hilary?"

I put out my hand. "You must be Alan! It's really nice to meet you." We shook hands quite formally.

"What would you like to do?" Alan asked. "Would you like to go somewhere for a meal?"

"That would be lovely." We decided to go to Hendersons, where we had a delicious meal. Alan talked a lot about his work in the outskirts of Glasgow, where he helped young people with drug and alcohol problems through rehabilitation. He seemed to really care about the people with whom he worked and I was finding myself drawn by his passion for those in need.

After the meal, we were walking along George Street when Alan suddenly began leap-frogging over all the parking meters. It made me laugh and I ran alongside him all the way down the street which, fortunately, was fairly empty by that time in the evening.

"What would you like to do now?"

I wasn't sure. I didn't want the evening to end just yet; we were getting on so well.

"Would you like to see where I live?" he asked.

"How far away is it?" I was feeling a little doubtful.

"It's only about 40 miles. It's this side of Glasgow."

"OK," I said. I had nothing to lose. We found his car, and Alan was the perfect gentleman, opening my door first. He was scoring a lot of brownie points this evening.

We drove off together and I couldn't help feeling the thrill of adventure. I knew that I was taking a risk, but at last I had someone to take a risk with.

At Alan's home, a ground floor flat on a small estate, he made some coffee and put on some music. "Would you like to dance?"

We were swept up in the emotion of two lonely people finding one another. I felt intoxicated by his kisses, and a warning light started flashing at the back of my mind: "Remember the checklist, remember the checklist." I struggled to remember what was on the list. I pulled gently away from his arms.

"Do you think the coffee is ready now?"

"Do you really want any coffee? Wouldn't you like something a little stronger?"

"No, thank you. Coffee would be just lovely."

We sat on the settee. "Alan, there are just a few things I would like to ask you."

"Yes."

"My faith is very important to me. Are you a Christian?"

Alan flinched slightly. "Well, I do go to church sometimes. Perhaps you could be a good influence on me?"

"Another thing: I don't believe in sex before marriage. What do you think about that?"

"I applaud people who have strong morals. After all, that is what I spend my life trying to teach others." He smiled. "Any more bombshells?"

"I never drink alcohol on a first date."

"Fair enough. We'll just have to wait until next time, then. Come on, let's dance again."

We did, and the hours passed blissfully.

"I really do need to get home," I said eventually.

"OK, as long as you promise to see me again soon."

We drove home in the early hours of the morning. It was raining slightly as we pulled up outside the flats. "I'll call you tomorrow," he said. I blew him a kiss and hurried in out of the rain.

Running up the stairs, I was bowled over by the first flush of love. It had really happened to me – I had met someone lovely. I was indescribably happy.

The next day, Alan rang and we arranged to go ice skating together that evening. He hadn't told me beforehand that he was an ace on the ice and I soon found myself whizzed around the rink, holding tightly to his hand, whilst my ankles buckled under the strain. We seemed to spend the entire evening laughing. The feelings of the previous night only seemed to intensify, the more we spent time together.

Within a few weeks, Alan was expressing the desire that our relationship should become more serious. It was at this point that he let me know that he was in the process of getting a divorce. I was shocked and began to wonder if there was anything else he had not yet told me. He was also finding the physical limitations which I had imposed on our relationship difficult and was putting increasing pressure on me to give in and have sex with him.

I felt as though I was in an impossible situation. My feelings for him were very strong. I had fallen in love, hook, line and sinker, but I wanted to honour the Lord and not have sex before marriage. Alan proposed to me and said that his divorce would be through very soon. I wanted to marry him, but the conflicts were becoming too great. I was forced to choose between fulfilling my sexual longings, and honouring the God who loved me so completely.

In the end, I had to tell Alan that I could not marry him and that our relationship would have to end. He asked me why and said that he still wanted to marry me. I explained the conflict and how difficult it had all become. He became bitter and angry, and asked for all the gifts that he had given me to be sent back.

I wrapped them up in a large bundle, posted them, and spent the night listening to a Neil Diamond tape on my personal cassette player. "Love on the Rocks" seemed to sum up the situation completely. After an hour and a half in a hot shower, and seven hours of continuous crying, I was ready to explain to my friends that my first love affair had come to an end.

Chapter Twenty-Seven

The ending of my relationship with Alan heralded the opportunity to re-evaluate the direction of my life. I felt wounded to the core of my being by our split, but in my heart of hearts I knew that I had done the right thing.

Nonetheless, I felt restless. CCU continued to challenge me professionally and I was doing my best to rise to that challenge, but all the time there was this feeling that I needed to be moving on. A reading from my daily Bible notes seemed to leap out from the page. It read: "Arise and go. This is no longer your place of rest" (Micah 2:10). I kept praying that the Lord would show me where I should be looking for this change of direction.

It came in the next edition of the *Nursing Times* magazine: a small advertisement offering midwifery tuition in Welwyn Garden City in Hertfordshire. As soon as I saw it, I felt an assurance that this was the place. I had not wanted to go to London, because it is such a large city, but I wanted to move south in order to be closer to my sisters, so Welwyn was the ideal place.

I wrote a letter of application and, having completed the appropriate forms, was invited for an interview, the date of which just happened to coincide with my next week's holiday, in March.

Walking around the hospital, I was delighted to see that it was far more modern than the Infirmary. The Maternity Unit was on the fifth floor and offered clean and modern amenities to the patients there. The interview itself was promising, because I was called by my first name and I felt a sense of belonging straightaway. I was delighted when they offered me a place on the next course, which was due to commence in May.

Returning to Edinburgh once again, I was aware that an era was coming to an end. Shahida and Judith had both applied for midwifery training at St Thomas' in London and had been accepted; they would be starting there in July. Suddenly, all our futures were about to change, but, in spite of the sadness of being parted from my dearest friends, I felt a strange peace that this was what I was supposed to do.

The final couple of months on CCU went slowly. I felt as though I was marking time; a lot of my enthusiasm for my work seemed to have ebbed away. My heart was already winging its way south and preparing for new adventures.

Before that happened, however, I had one last week's holiday to take and I took it at a retreat house in the south-west of England. The brochure had advertised a prayer week for those interested in becoming effective in prayer.

Turning up on a damp and cold Monday afternoon, I was welcomed, along with 59 other people, to a beautiful old mansion which stood in acres of its own grounds. I was allocated a room, sharing with two other young women and, after unpacking, we went downstairs to prepare for the first seminar.

I didn't really know quite what to expect, but I had that strange feeling that God was about to do something special. The speaker was talking about prayer and saying that when we learn how to really pray, then God can act very powerfully.

I sat there, nodding and smiling, thinking, Yes, this is really good. Gradually, the speaker moved on to explain that we need the anointing of the Holy Spirit if we are truly to engage in spiritual warfare, overcoming the powers of darkness, in the name of Jesus. I began to get that uncomfortable feeling when you suddenly realise that God has far more planned for you than you thought.

At the Chapel in Edinburgh, talk about the Holy Spirit and exercising some of the gifts of the Spirit, for example, speaking in tongues, had been looked upon with distrust. Over the past few months, though, I had had this longing to move on in my faith, to become an effective person of prayer, and this speaker was making perfect sense. The gift of tongues, he explained, helped us to pray in tune with the Holy Spirit, in a way which was even more effective than if we simply prayed into situations with our own limited human understanding.

At the end of his talk, the speaker simply said, "Are there any here today who have never spoken in tongues?"

Part of me wanted to bolt for the door. The other part found my arm waving in the breeze, indicating that I was such a person.

Almost immediately, I was surrounded by a group of strangers who were praying that I should receive this gift. I sat there in the middle, feeling very embarrassed, not knowing what on earth to do.

After a while, I listened to the others praying and I kept opening and shutting my mouth like a goldfish, but no sound would come out. If God wanted to give me a gift, then I definitely wanted it, but nothing seemed to be happening.

A woman sitting beside me said, "Don't worry, just relax and let God give you the words."

So I sat there a while longer, as they all continued praying. It was getting really embarrassing now. I couldn't think of anything to say, so I returned to the goldfish impersonations.

The woman beside me held my hand. "Just make a sound, and then God can use that," she said.

So I tried making a sound in my throat, but it was croaky and very quiet. I was getting desperate by now, but I persevered and started saying, "La la la". I felt such a fool and utterly drained by the entire experience.

"That's it! Well done!" the woman said. The group obviously thought that this was the signal for them to stop praying. They left for the dining room, leaving me feeling a fraud.

Later on, whilst taking a bath, I suddenly felt a tremendous peace and joy, so I started singing. It was a few minutes before I realised that I was no longer singing in English, but in a new and very beautiful language that I had never heard before.

Once again, the Lord had broken through into my life in a way that I could not have imagined possible. The rest of the week was spent learning how to engage in prayer; it was a time of tremendous blessing.

On the final day, we were praying for God to speak to us, so that we would be sent out with a clear picture of his will for us. Whilst we were praying, I saw in my mind's eye a picture of two people surrounded by a gold ring, turning and walking through a gate which was opening ahead of them.

We were asked to come to the front and describe the pictures we had received, but I was so frightened, that I did not want to speak in front of all these very strong and mature people. My heart started thudding as person after person explained that the Lord had been speaking to them about the sanctity of marriage and how he wanted to help couples to reach out to others in their communities.

"Is there anyone else with something to say?"

Oh, no, I thought, I'm going to have to do this. My leaden arm found its way above my head.

"Please, stand up and tell us what it is you have to say," said the speaker.

I stood up and started to speak, but I could barely hear myself, let alone be heard by the other people in the room.

"Come up here and use the microphone."

Oh, no, that's even worse, I thought. But I went to the front and, blushing and stammering, described the picture I had seen. When I had finished, the speaker smiled and said, "Well, isn't that typical of our Lord, to save the best till last?"

I came to the conclusion then and there that God does not always make it easy for us to follow him and that he often uses our weaknesses to bring important messages to others. With this in mind, I travelled north for the last time, in readiness to begin a week of night duty on CCU.

As usual, the unit was busy and full. On the first night, I was allocated two patients, one of whom was an elderly man who had experienced a heart attack at home and then had suffered a cardiac arrest just before the paramedics had arrived. He was consequently very confused, owing to the hypoxia, or low levels of oxygen reaching his brain, during those few precarious minutes before the paramedics managed to restart his heart.

Alistair was particularly challenging because he could not understand why he was in a strange bed, surrounded by equipment which bleeped and whirred all night. The late shift had resorted to using restraints to prevent him from pulling out his drip and removing the cardiac electrodes from his chest, which he had managed to do some five times since admission. Consequently, his hands were lightly bandaged to the cot sides.

My other patient, Derek, was a middle-aged man who suffered from unstable angina and who was being observed whilst new medication was being offered. He was well whilst at rest, but the slightest exertion brought on severe chest pain.

Walking into Alistair's room first, I introduced myself and checked that all of his observations were satisfactory. All seemed well, fluid balance was fine, and the urinary catheter was running clear. I dimmed the light switch slightly to help him settle down to sleep. He seemed peaceful enough, so I passed on into Derek's room.

"Good evening, Derek. My name is Hilary and I am looking after you this evening. How are you feeling?"

He turned a cheerfully chubby face towards me. "Och, I'm hunky-dory, Nurse, thank you."

"Sister said that you have been experiencing a lot of pain whenever you move about, is that right?"

"Och, well, it's a wee bit of a bugger is that. But I'm all right when I'm sitting still. I can still do my crossword, so there's no need to complain."

"The new drugs which you are trying will hopefully help you to have less pain, but they may take a little while to work."

"Aye, so the top doc said. What's his name again?"

"Professor Mulberry."

"Aye, that's it. Nice man, but a bit on the formal side, if you ken what I mean. Why doesn't someone tell him that he always forgets to fold down the collar on his white coat? Otherwise, he's quite respectablelooking."

I laughed. "The consultants always wear their coat collars up to show that they are consultants. It's like a badge of office."

"Well, blow me down! I shall have to tell the wife that. She thought he was a bit dodgy because of that. Och well, it just goes to show you, doesn't it?"

"It most certainly does. Can I just check your blood pressure again, just to make sure that you're set fair for the night?"

"Of course you can, my love. Anything for a pretty nurse."

His observations were all normal and his ECG looked fine. I dimmed his lights for him and settled his pillows and sheets so that he was as comfortable as possible.

"I'll have to keep coming in to check on you during the night, but your buzzer is just here if you need me at any time."

"Thanks, Nurse. Good night."

"Good night, Derek. Sleep well."

I left the room and went to the station to write up my

nursing notes for Alistair and Derek. The other nurses were all doing the same.

"Looks like Alistair may be getting a bit restless, Hilary." It was Sister Bowman. She was tall and elegant, and had an aura of peace about her which brought calm to the most chaotic of situations. She had the ability to put everyone at ease and, of all the senior staff on the unit, she was my favourite.

"I'll just go and see if he's all right."

I leapt up from the stool and walked briskly into Alistair's room. It took a second for my eyes to readjust, but I could see that he was wriggling and writhing in his bed. I turned up the lights slightly.

"It's OK, Alistair. I'm here to help you."

"Go away!" he screamed. "I don't know you!" He was writhing frantically at this stage and I didn't see until it was too late that he had managed to free his left hand from the restraints. The next moment, an impressive left hook was landing on my right cheek. I recoiled in shock and horror, and tried to take hold of the hand before it did any more damage.

Sister Bowman came into the room. "Are you all right, Hilary? I saw what happened."

I felt a surge of relief, accompanied by resentment.

"I'm all right, thank you. Is there something we could give Alistair to help him to calm down? This level of agitation can't be doing his heart any favours."

"I'll call the registrar. They really should have prescribed sedation earlier."

She recaptured Alistair's flailing arm and expertly restrained it once again. Her aura of peace seemed even to touch Alistair's troubled spirits.

I stayed with Alistair until the registrar had come and administered sedation intravenously. Within a few minutes, peace was returning. With the peace came a nagging ache on my face. As I left the room for the nurses' station there were "oohs" and "aahs" of sympathy from my colleagues.

"That's gonnae be a shiner in the morning." It was Martyn's attempt at moral support. At one o'clock in the morning, however, all I wanted was a cup of hot chocolate and a nice long sleep.

"You'd better go for your break now," said Sister Bowman, "whilst the coast is clear. They all seem fairly settled at the moment and you could probably do with putting a cold compress on that cheek of yours."

"Thank you, Sister."

I took my handbag from the locker under the nurses' station and headed for the door. From past experience, I knew that a few minutes of walking down the long corridors would help to clear my head and sort out the subjective feelings of shock, from the objective ideas on how to better manage a similar incident in the future.

It was very quiet in the canteen, so I took my mug of hot chocolate and sat at a corner table. As usual at this time in the morning, the canteen carpet began to wobble and swirl before my eyes. I am convinced that very few people are born to work all night.

I drank the hot chocolate slowly, and deliberately made myself relax in the chair. It was an attempt to dig deeply into my reserves of energy and concentration. I knew that once back in the unit, I would have to be alert and functioning well.

"The next three hours will be the worst and then it will get better," I said to myself. The worst hours of the night are between 2 a.m. and 5 a.m., when everyone's circadian rhythm is at a low ebb. This means that, not only do many patients die during this crucial period of the night, but the people looking after them are also battling with their own internal time clocks and are forcing themselves to function when their body is crying out for sleep.

I checked my fob watch every two minutes and made sure

that I took at least 25 of the 30 minutes of my break. Taking a few deep breaths, I left the canteen and walked briskly down the deserted corridor back to the unit.

Walking through the doors, I fully expected to see at least one resuscitation in progress, but all was quiet and still. Sister Bowman was vigilantly watching all ten screens and talking quietly to Martyn. She turned to me. "You were quick! Are you sure you took your full half-hour?"

"Yes, I'm fine. It was so quiet in the canteen that I might have fallen asleep."

"How's the cheek?"

"Oh, it's OK. I'll have to learn to dodge next time."

I was bending down to replace my handbag in the locker when one of the alarms sounded.

"It's Derek! He's gone into VF."

I stared at the screen in disbelief. "He can't have!"

But the evidence was all too clear. The screen showed the chaotic gyrations of a heart in total disarray. I grabbed the crash trolley and moved quickly into Derek's room. There was always a part of me which hoped beyond hope that perhaps it was just a loose connection with the monitor, or a wonky electrode. But as I entered the room, Derek was convulsing as his heart was unable to circulate an adequate blood supply to his brain.

I quickly laid him flat and charged up the defibrillator paddles. I placed pads containing conductor gel on to Derek's chest and, as the defibrillator beeped to confirm that it was ready for action, I said, "Shocking! Stand clear!"

Derek's arms twitched slightly as the charge entered his body. Sister and I watched the monitor anxiously to see if there would be a return to normal sinus rhythm. The monitor continued to spew out its horrific trace.

"Increase to 200, Hilary." Sister Bowman was administering oxygen via an airway and ambubag.

"OK." I adjusted the dial quickly and set the defibrillator to charge.

"Stand clear! Shocking!"

Derek's arms and shoulders convulsed briefly, but the monitor confirmed that there was no change in cardiac activity.

"Come on, Derek, I know you can do this!" I half whispered, as the defibrillator beeped once again. "I've increased to 360, Sister."

"That's fine. The anaesthetist is here. You carry on."

"Shocking!" This time the trace showed complete asystole – Derek's heart was now completely still.

"We need some atropine and adrenalin by the look of things." It was Dr Crawshaw, looking as though he had just fallen out of a haystack.

I left the paddles of the defibrillator and quickly drew up some atropine and adrenalin, checking them with Sister Bowman. Dr Crawshaw administered the drugs intravenously. He then went on to intubate Derek to ensure that as much oxygen as possible was circulating in his bloodstream.

We all watched the monitor, willing there to be a return to a healthy rhythm, but the monitor showed a complete absence of any cardiac activity. I began cardiac compressions, depressing Derek's chest five times and pausing for the anaesthetist to fill his lungs with oxygen once again.

We repeated the intravenous medication, but to no avail. Derek's heart could no longer beat and, after 40 minutes of attempted resuscitation, Dr Crawshaw announced that his life was over.

I closed my eyes for a second and prayed for Derek and his wife. I could feel the waves of disappointment and sadness crashing in an almost physical way into my mind. An overwhelming fatigue seemed to seat itself upon my shoulders as I began the clearing up of the room and the performance of last offices.

As with all failed resuscitations, there was an awful sense of sadness and defeat. Why did people have to die? It all seemed so unfair. Just a few hours ago, Derek had been laughing and joking with me. The book of crosswords under his bed reminded me of the man who had just passed away – full of life and, more importantly perhaps, always seeing the funny side of things.

I washed his body gently and combed his hair. Sister Bowman had already phoned his wife to let her know of her husband's death and we were expecting her to arrive any minute. When she did, I escorted her into her husband's room. I left her sitting by his side, telling him all the things that she needed to say so that their parting could begin.

She sat there for about an hour, quietly talking and kissing his cooling hand. Eventually, she stood up and, kissing Derek on his lips for the last time, walked slowly out of the room.

"Thank you, Nurse, for everything."

"I'm so very sorry. Your husband was a wonderful man."

"Yes," she said. "Yes, he was one in a million."

With that, she squeezed my hand and walked quickly out of the unit.

Chapter Twenty-Eight

The week of night duty eventually came to an end and I felt that, at last, I had become more objective about dealing with life and death. Sister Bowman had commented that I now performed like an experienced CCU nurse and no longer like a frightened rabbit, which aptly described my behaviour when I had first arrived in the unit.

In the remaining week on day duty, I was given the honour of taking charge of the whole unit for one shift, with Sister Bellamy working as my junior and able to step into the breech should anything untoward happen.

Once again, I was terrified of the responsibility. I wasn't sure which worried me the most – dealing with very ill patients, or dealing with the various consultants! My prayers were answered on the day in question, because it was a relatively quiet shift, with only one admission, and the rest of the patients behaved very well.

In the remaining few days, I was allocated Mr Shaw as my patient. He was 69 years old and we were having great difficulty in stabilising his heart condition. His heart would go into ventricular tachycardia, VT, where the larger chambers of his heart, the ventricles, would be pumping too fast to allow an adequate blood supply to circulate. It always seemed to happen that he would go into VT at three o'clock in the afternoon and would need shocking with the defibrillator to help his heart return to a normal rhythm.

On the day after he was admitted, it was Mr Shaw's 70th birthday; Sister had brought a cake into the unit for him.

We all sang "Happy Birthday" around his bed and he blew out the candle – and promptly went into VT once again.

On the third day, he had been very stable all morning and said that he was feeling very comfortable. All was well, until three o'clock. As soon as I saw the trace, I grabbed the crash trolley and headed for his room. He had convulsed so that his upper body was in danger of falling out of the bed.

I grasped his hand and I will never forget the strength of his hand in mine. I was panting with the effort of moving his body back on to the bed. A jug of water had been knocked to the floor and I slipped on one of the pillows which had been thrown there in our haste. I wondered if he was aware of the struggle. Laying him flat, I proceeded to perform a sternal thump, which can have the same effect as a small electrical charge and can sometimes be enough to revert the heart's rhythm back to normal.

Looking quickly at the monitor, I could see that this wasn't going to work this time. I slipped in an airway and applied an ambubag and started to ventilate him. Sister Carrey continued with the defibrillator.

We fought hard to revive Mr Shaw, but this time we were unsuccessful. The fact that we had shared his birthday celebrations seemed to make his death even more poignant. The rest of the unit was busy, so I was left, once again, to perform last offices on my own.

"I'm so sorry that we could not help you this time, Mr Shaw," I said as I washed his feet. "I pray that God will guide you to a place of wonderful peace and rest."

I then combed his hair and did something that I had never done before: I leaned forward and kissed him gently on his forehead.

"He looks very peaceful, Hilary." Sister Carrey was standing behind me; I hadn't heard her enter the room and I felt embarrassed.

"Don't worry," she said. "We need to love our patients; otherwise, what kind of nurses would we be?"

The following day, I received a letter asking me to attend the nursing officers' office. It was the day I had been dreaming of for the past four years.

Dear Staff Nurse McIntosh,

It has come to our attention that you have completed your year as a staff nurse at the Royal Infirmary of Edinburgh, following your training here, and that you are now entitled to receive your hospital badge. Please attend at the above office at 10 a.m.

Walking towards the dark oak doors once again, I thought back to all the times I had met with my fate in this very place. From the first time, when I had been so much younger and so full of ideals, to the times when I had had to face up to my fears of death, failure, rejection, and even the dark. And now, I stood here on the brink of receiving the prize for which I had grafted, sweated and wept.

My palms were moist once again as I lifted my hand to knock on the door.

"Come!"

I stepped into the room.

"Ah, Staff Nurse McIntosh. This is a very splendid day."

"Thank you."

"Well, I suppose we shouldn't beat about the bush."

The nursing officer opened the drawer in her desk and brought out a small blue velvet box. Opening it, she checked the name on the back of the badge inside.

"It gives me great pleasure to present you with the Pelican badge. I trust that you will always wear it with pride."

I gazed at the silver and blue badge nestling in my hand. For all my attempts at feigning indifference and maturity, I felt a lump in my throat the size of a gobstopper. Here, in my hand, lay the badge which symbolised all the effort of the past four years. All the trials and tribulations, all the bullying and failures, all the tender moments with patients and their relatives – all the lives which I had been privileged to share.

"Thank you so much."

"Off you go now."

"Yes. Thank you so much."

I almost bowed as I turned to walk out of the door. My hands were shaking as I tried to pin the badge to my uniform, but eventually, it was in place and I walked back to CCU, thanking God for all that he had brought me through.

Two days later, Shahida, Judith and I were packed into a taxi along with all my worldly belongings – they had come to see me off.

"We need to make sure you leave the premises, Hilary!" Shahida was laughing.

"Don't worry, Shahida. I really am going."

We stood on the platform at Waverley Station, hopping up and down and blowing on our hands. A lazy wind was blowing from the north, but the sun was bright. I looked at Shahida. "This will be you in a couple of months."

"I know and I can't wait."

"Och, it's not been that bad, surely?" Judith was grinning widely. She knew just how bad it had been.

The guard walked up and down the platform.

"Well, I guess this is it. Thank you so much for all your love and help, Shahida."

The three of us made a hug sandwich and then we wrestled the suitcase and trunk on to the train.

"We'll be in touch."

I found my seat and, waving madly out of the window, watched as the platform slowly slipped away. Shahida and Judith were still waving as their features became indistinguishable.

I sat back in my seat and watched as the beautiful Scottish hills gave way to the flatter land of England. I felt that I was crossing to another promised land. All that had gone before, so beautifully depicted in the picture of the pelican sacrificing itself in order to feed its young, had given me a lifetime's supply of memories, which had changed me forever.

Exactly what lay ahead I could not tell, but at least this time, I was going in the knowledge that I was not alone and that the Lord would be with me, guarding and guiding me all the way.

Glossary

Abbreviations:

APH   antepartum haemorrhage
CPR   cardio pulmonary resuscitation
CVA   cerebral vascular accident (or stroke)
IV   intravenous
IVI   intravenous infusion
LSCS   lower segment Caesarean section
SHO   senior house officer

Terms used:

Brachial artery	An artery on the inside of the elbow
Echo scan	A form of scan using ultra sound
Theatre pack	When the sheets and blankets are folded in such a way to facilitate covering the patient following surgery
Thrombolytic therapy	Drugs which break down blood clots
Venflon	A fine needle and tube inserted into a vein in order to administer drugs intravenously
Y graft	A graft which is inserted into the aorta where it divides to supply blood to each of the legs. The graft replaces the damaged blood vessel, and is an upside-down "y" shape